Pedagogies

Popular Music Pedagogies: A Practical Guide for Music Teachers provides readers with a solid foundation of playing and teaching a variety of instruments and technologies, and then examines how these elements work together in a comprehensive school music program. With individual chapters designed to stand independently, instructors can adapt this guide to a range of learning abilities and teaching situations by combining the pedagogies and methodologies presented. This textbook is an ideal resource for preservice music educators enrolled in popular music education, modern band, or secondary general methods coursework and K-12 music teachers who wish to create or expand popular music programs in their schools. The website includes play-alongs, video demonstrations, printed materials, and links to useful popular music pedagogy resources.

Matthew Clauhs, PhD is an Assistant Professor of Music Education at Ithaca College where he teaches wind methods and modern band.

Bryan Powell, DMA is an Assistant Professor of Music Education and Music Technology at Montclair State University.

Ann C. Clements, PhD is Professor of Music Education and Director of the Center for Pedagogy in Arts and Design at the Pennsylvania State University.

Popular Music Pedagogies

A Practical Guide for Music Teachers

MATTHEW CLAUHS,
BRYAN POWELL, AND
ANN C. CLEMENTS

Routledge
Taylor & Francis Group

NEW YORK AND LONDON

First published 2021
by Routledge
52 Vanderbilt Avenue, New York, NY 10017

and by Routledge
2 Park Square, Milton Park, Abingdon, Oxon OX14 4RN

Routledge is an imprint of the Taylor & Francis Group, an informa business

© 2021 Taylor & Francis

The right of Matthew Clauhs, Bryan Powell and Ann C. Clements to be identified as authors of this work has been asserted by them in accordance with sections 77 and 78 of the Copyright, Designs and Patents Act 1988.

Paperback and eBook covers: Left circle image – Brenda Montalbano – Photo Credit DIME Detroit; Right top image – Steve Holley's music ensemble – Photo Credit Carol MacKay; Right bottom image – Tony Corallo's music class– Photo credit Tony Corallo.

Trademark notice: Product or corporate names may be trademarks or registered trademarks, and are used only for identification and explanation without intent to infringe.

Library of Congress Cataloging-in-Publication Data
Names: Clauhs, Matthew, author. | Powell, Bryan, author. |
Clements, Ann Callistro, author.
Title: Popular music pedagogies: a practical guide for music
teachers / Matthew Clauhs, Bryan Powell, and Ann C. Clements.
Description: New York : Routledge, 2021. |
Includes bibliographical references and index.
Identifiers: LCCN 2020030095 (print) | LCCN 2020030096 (ebook) |
ISBN 9780367266578 (hardback) | ISBN 9780367266585 (paperback) |
ISBN 9780429294440 (ebook)
Subjects: LCSH: Popular music–Instruction and study. |
School music–Instruction and study.
Classification: LCC MT10 .C615 2021 (print) |
LCC MT10 (ebook) | DDC 780.71–dc23
LC record available at https://lccn.loc.gov/2020030095
LC ebook record available at https://lccn.loc.gov/2020030096

ISBN: 978-0-367-26657-8 (hbk)
ISBN: 978-0-367-26658-5 (pbk)
ISBN: 978-0-429-29444-0 (ebk)

Typeset in Sabon
by Newgen Publishing UK

Visit the companion website: www.popmusicped.com

To our families that support us and our students who inspire us.

CONTENTS

LIST OF FIGURES

PREFACE

Popular Music Pedagogies: A Practical Guide for Music Teachers provides readers with a solid foundation of playing and teaching a variety of instruments and technologies before examining how these elements work together in a comprehensive school music program. The chapters in this book are designed to be independent, meaning readers can select which material is most relevant to their unique teaching situations. For example, readers who do not intend to teach ukulele may skip that chapter without fear of missing information that is necessary to understand other chapters. However, we recommend reading Chapter 2: Introduction to Guitar, Bass, and Ukulele before exploring those individual instrument chapters. We organized the material this way because there is no standard instrumentation or set of technological tools for popular music education, and whatever exists now will soon evolve or may become obsolete. We believe that readers will be able to teach popular music successfully with any combination of the instruments and/or technologies presented in this book.

The textbook begins by exploring the foundations of popular music education, examining the philosophical and pedagogical underpinnings of this movement. The remainder of the textbook is organized into three parts: Instrument Techniques, Music Technology, and Putting It All Together. While a linear progression through the textbook may make sense for some readers, the material is not presented sequentially, so readers may explore the book however it works best for their individual contexts. Part I: Instrument Techniques demonstrates how to play and teach each instrument at a beginning to intermediate level in a classroom or ensemble format using iconic notation (e.g., **chord diagrams**, pictures, and tablature) and accessible approaches to engage a variety of learners. This part begins with an introduction to the fretted instruments most common in popular music education: guitar, bass, and ukulele, and presents forms of notation and techniques that are shared among these instruments. The next two chapters explore principles of guitar and ukulele performance in greater depth and lead the reader through strumming patterns and chord progression activities. The following chapter includes approaches to playing and teaching bass lines in a variety of styles. The chapter titled Keyboard focuses on movable hand shapes, comping patterns, and the different possibilities for incorporating this instrument into a popular music ensemble. Next, the reader learns approaches to body percussion, the basic rock beat, and fills in the drum kit chapter. The final chapter of Part I, Vocals, includes singing techniques and considerations for teaching voice in popular music contexts. Each chapter outlines performance techniques unique to the instrument and offers suggestions for **differentiation** to accommodate learners of various abilities and experience levels. In addition to vocal pedagogy, we selected guitar, electric bass, keyboard, drum kit, and ukulele because they are the most common acoustic and electronic instruments for teaching popular music in the United States, due in large part to the rapid expansion of modern band classes and ensembles in recent years.

Part II: Music Technology comprises the following chapters: Apps and Software, Digital Audio Workstations, and Live Sound and Recording. While the instrumentation outlined in Part I is typical of many popular music ensembles, the most widely consumed form of music today, hip hop, is often orchestrated exclusively with synthesizers, sequencers, and other digital instruments such as drum machines and digital audio workstations (DAWs). Therefore, Part II of the textbook examines how these tools may be used to produce, record, and share student music either in conjunction with or separate from the instruments of Part I, depending on the teaching situation and style of music. The first chapter on apps/software is a survey of tools available for iOS, Android, Chrome, MacOS, and Windows operating systems that are useful to the popular music education teacher and student. The focus of the chapter is on the practical application of the tools in a music classroom and is not a how-to guide on the specific apps and software. This chapter provides sample activities for creating and arranging music of any style on any school budget. The second chapter explores how DAWs may function as an instrument for live performance, as a tool for music production, and as a means for recording live performances. The goal of this chapter is to examine how these tools facilitate creativity and collaboration in popular music education. The third chapter, Live Sound and Recording, explains how audio equipment works and functions in popular music classrooms, studios, and performance spaces, covering everything from cables and connectors to mixers and PA systems. Many music educators struggle with the technical aspects of operating audio equipment or designing optimal performing and recording spaces. This chapter provides ideas for rehearsal rooms, performance spaces, collaborative stations, and recording studios with jargon-free language. In this chapter, readers learn how to get the best possible sound out of their classroom equipment.

The final section, Part III: Putting It All Together, connects instrumental techniques and digital technologies to praxis through a series of chapters: Making the Band; Songwriting, Improvisation, and Arranging; and Hip Hop. The first chapter, Making the Band, presents strategies for democratic decision-making and collaboration in a performance-based ensemble. Readers will learn how to select repertoire together with students, facilitate rehearsals, and design significant learning experiences in a student-centered environment. The chapter includes a survey of suggested ensemble formats, drawing on combinations of the instruments and digital tools provided in Parts I and II of this textbook. The Songwriting, Improvisation, and Arranging chapter examines creative processes essential to a popular music program. Although creating music is one of the artistic processes guiding our National Core Arts

Standards for music education, many educators struggle to incorporate creative music-making experiences in the classroom. Teachers often favor activities that recreate the works of master composers – or cover songs, in the case of popular music pedagogy. In this chapter, readers learn how to design lessons that give students ownership of the creative process. The final chapter, Hip Hop, presents strategies for teaching the most widely consumed musical genre in the United States, with an emphasis on making beats, **freestyling**, and writing lyrics.

The authors of *Popular Music Pedagogies* recognize that some of the learning activities presented in this textbook may not be appropriate for all learners and accommodations should be made whenever possible. Each chapter includes a section on differentiation to identify strategies that engage all learners through popular music education. There are references throughout *Popular Music Pedagogies* to a website created by the authors, http://popmusicped.com, that is specifically designed for readers of this textbook. The website includes videos and links to supplement this textbook with relevant examples of playing and teaching popular music. The authors will update this online resource regularly with the performance techniques, lesson plans, and the latest resources available to popular music educators. We encourage readers to submit their own cases and experiences with popular music education through the website and contribute to the growing body of field-tested best practices. Through this practice, http://popmusicped.com will become a resource cocreated by practitioners of popular music education.

Although the popular music education movement is widespread across the United States, few music teacher practitioners have a strong background in the instrument techniques, music technologies, and pedological approaches necessary to teach popular music classes and ensembles with a high degree of success. This is largely because music teacher education programs rarely include this content in their curricula. We hope that K-12 educators and preservice music teacher educators who are engaging students with popular music find this textbook to be a valuable resource as they develop proficiencies on the instruments and technologies applicable to their teaching situation and broaden their understandings of the contexts and practical applications of these techniques. We also hope that preservice music educators taking coursework in popular music pedagogies or general music methods find this textbook useful as they consider the potential for popular music in their future classrooms.

Music educators at every level should strive to keep up with current trends in popular music performance and work collaboratively with students to plan and implement curricular changes at regular intervals. All educational work in popular music runs the risk of becoming outdated and this book is no exception. However, the pedagogies described within are not connected to a specific genre or popular style of music-making, allowing the flexibility to maintain relevance regardless of what is trending. We hope that the readers of this book are prepared to adapt to the changing landscape of popular music education.

Preface

Indeed, student-centered pedagogy will always remain current because our students are always current. For this reason, we emphasize approach and instructional delivery, not specific content or repertoire. Techniques learned in this textbook should be applicable to new instrumentations and technologies. Readers should also remember that they do not need to follow this textbook in a sequential manner. The book is designed as a *choose your own adventure* in popular music education, recognizing that every classroom will look, sound, and feel different, depending on the individual needs and learning goals of the students in that space. Readers may also decide the depth to which they wish to go for each chapter, by engaging in more or less of the supplementary material found at http://popmusicped.com.

We hope readers receive these ideas with an open mind to the ever-expanding possibilities of music education. The approaches described here may be unchartered territory for many, and music teachers in popular music classrooms will certainly make mistakes along the way. Readers are encouraged to apply a growth mindset when practicing these ideas – for themselves and for their current or future students. There is often a degree of perceived chaos in student-centered work, and music educators need to practice being comfortable with the messiness of creativity. The field of popular music education will take time to develop, but the authors are encouraged by the trajectory of this movement in recent years. By providing culturally responsive and learner-centered opportunities through popular music education, we may begin to reach an overarching goal of inclusive and creative music-making experiences for all students.

ACKNOWLEDGMENTS

There are many teachers and scholars doing excellent work in the areas of popular music education, democratic practice, and informal music learning. We are particularly grateful for the expertise of Beatrice Olesko, Jesse Rathgeber, Colin Sapp, Tiger Robison, Cassandra Eisenreich, Chris Venesile, Gareth Dylan Smith, Kat Reinhert, Radio Cremata, Jonathan Kladder, Brian Franco, Steve Holley, Kris Gilbert, and Ian Cummings, all of whom provided valuable feedback on chapter drafts for this book. We would also like to thank James Eldreth for his assistance with bibliographies and formatting, Warren Gramm for copyediting assistance, and Bridget Toolan for the artwork and graphics throughout this book and at http://popmusicped.com.

We would like to acknowledge the Little Kids Rock nonprofit organization for leading the charge in popular music education and modern band, making culturally relevant music education accessible to all students. By providing instruments to underserved students and professional development and free resources to music teachers across the United States, Little Kids Rock has inspired a movement toward inclusive music education that meets the needs of an increasingly diverse (by race, class, and musical preference) body of students. This organization has challenged the notion of a one-size-fits-all paradigm for school music education by broadening the curriculum and listening to voices of often marginalized student populations. A portion of proceeds from this book will be donated to the Little Kids Rock nonprofit organization to support this cause. We encourage readers to visit http://littlekidsrock.org to learn more about the tremendous impact of this organization.

On a personal note, the authors wish to thank the following individuals for their love and support along our popular music education journeys.

From Matthew: I would like to thank the students, faculty, and staff at Ithaca College for creating an innovative, collaborative, and endlessly supportive learning environment. I am especially grateful to my peer mentors, the junior squad: Ben, Sean, Beatrice, and Jonathan, for their friendship and guidance through early career challenges and opportunities. And my infinite gratitude and love to my wife Laura, who inspires me in every aspect of life.

From Bryan: I would like to thank the many people who have been integral in my popular music education journey, especially Robin, Dunbar, Edd, Harold, Joe, Andy, Lee, Radio, Susan, Dave, Scott, Steve, and Gareth. Thank you to my collegial coauthors Matt and Ann; I enjoyed the journey with you both. And as always, my love to Liz, Ellison, and Beckett, without whom things would have significantly less meaning.

From Ann: I would like to thank the many wonderful music educators around the world who have championed the inclusion of popular music in schools. It is their pioneering work that has made this book possible. I would also like to thank each of you who have decided to read a copy, as I believe doing so will create new musical opportunities for your current or future students. It may even enhance your own music-making! A sincere thank you to my student James Eldreth who has contributed greatly to the organization of this book (and to so many aspects of my career). Lastly, I would like to thank my mother Alice Callistro for her continuing support of my musical development, my husband Chaz Wall for his assistance and encouragement that allows me to dedicate time and energy to these kinds of projects, and to my son Charles Wall who is the inspiration for all that I do.

Foundations of Popular Music Pedagogies

> While American music has clearly flourished and evolved over the last several decades, it's difficult to say the same for American music education.
>
> – Robert Woody[1]

We live in a time of rapid social, cultural, technological, economic, and political change. American music education is confronted with advancements in how people experience music and the ways in which children are educated.[2] While we have good reason to preserve our long-standing traditions in school music, there is a continuing concern with the apparent disconnect between school music and music as it exists within our world.[3] Young people have access to a limitless number of styles, genres, and approaches to learning music through digital streaming and online content. **Popular music**[4] remains exactly that – the most popular of all styles of music listened to, shared, emulated, and created by amateur and professional musicians. It can include music that is widely consumed by a large portion of the population or is characterized by amateur engagement, informality, a commitment to the process of making music, and a focus on pragmatic, "functional" musicianship skills that will serve students in a variety of ways.[5] In K-12 contexts, this music can include currently popular music, student songwriting, folk music, and music that is not commercially popular but is interesting to students.

With unprecedented cultural and technological growth comes an increased possibility for conflict and competition. At times, it can feel as though the profession has become two distinct camps consisting of those who are concerned with the maintenance of traditional ensembles and the curricular foundations of Western music history and notation, and those who are driven to engage in curricular reform that pushes the boundaries of democratic, culturally responsive music education. Tradition and modernization, which are too often viewed as opposite ends of a continuum, serve as a point of tension within the field as we consider future directions for school music. While some music teachers feel the profession is not moving fast enough toward the new, others believe that curricular expansion puts our traditional school music culture at risk.

The combination of tradition and modern presents meaningful and unique opportunities for learners to develop a large variety of musical skills while providing school music education to a larger number of students. Music education scholar Randall Allsup writes, "school music is more creative and more open than ever before, and more teachers are coming into the profession with a larger range of skills and the disposition to teach more imaginatively."[6] From this viewpoint, tradition and modernization can move forward together in a complementary trajectory to meet the needs of all students, including those for whom traditional practices have worked successfully and those who are less interested in school music offerings. Of course, many emerging methods are untested and may not work well in some situations, and not all traditions engage the interest and spirit of our students, thus, all school music is fertile ground for reflection and critique. Some of the strongest conversations surrounding change include (1) revisiting the relevancy of curricular offerings in regard to the needs and preferences of modern students, (2) the desire to reach a broader number of students, (3) expansion of performance offerings, (4) practices fostering democratic engagement that are inclusive and culturally responsive, and (5) an increase in creativity and collaboration through music arranging and composition. In order to address these challenges of change, music educators must reexamine current practices and consider how students are prepared for lifelong and life-wide musical experiences that transcend classroom walls.

POPULAR MUSIC PEDAGOGIES

If authentic production and transmission practices are missing from the curriculum and our teaching strategies, we will be dealing with a simulacrum, or a ghost of popular music in the classroom, and not the thing itself.

– Lucy Green[7]

The teaching practices that accompany the inclusion of popular music, hereon referred to as **popular music pedagogies** (PMPs), provide an opportunity for music teachers to utilize a multitude of approaches that change the dynamic of the traditional teacher–student power relationship. There is not a singular pedagogy to teaching popular music, but a range of approaches to fit a variety of popular music styles and genres. However, we believe there are enough commonalities within popular music teaching and learning to apply general principles. PMPs contain the design, practices, and approaches of learning popular music,[8] centering on **informal learning** and nonformal teaching practices.[9] Lucy Green, a well-known scholar of PMPs, defined the key tenets of informal learning as: (1) the learners choose music for themselves that they are familiar with and like; (2) the learners copy recordings by ear; (3) practice and refinement occur through self-learning, peer-directed learning, and group learning; (4) the learners focus on whole, "real-world" pieces of music; and (5) personal creativity is emphasized through the deep integration of listening, performing, improvising, and composing throughout the learning process.[10] The UK-based nonprofit music organization Musical Futures defined nonformal teaching as a pedagogical approach to learner-led instruction that includes:

> [a] fully inclusive approach to music making; group-based activities in performing, listening, composing and improvising; a sense of immediacy and exploration; tacit learning; music being caught not taught; music teachers/ leaders often play a lot, and explain very little, utilising skills within the group through peer learning, students and teachers co-constructing content; [and] opportunities to develop non-cognitive skills, such as responsibility, empathy, support for others, creativity and improvisation to find solutions.[11]

The instructional activities and descriptions of instrument technique utilized in this textbook will draw from these instructional approaches, which have been field-tested, researched, and currently accepted as pedagogies in popular music education.

Popular Music in Classrooms

While a thorough examination of the history of popular music in American schools is outside the scope of this book, it is helpful to understand the context of popular music in curriculum reform.[12] Current researchers and practitioners tend to cite the Tanglewood Declaration in 1967 and the directive that music education should include "currently popular teenage music"[13] as a turning point for the inclusion of popular music into the music education curriculum. The Tanglewood Symposium brought together music educators, composers, performers, and publishers to discuss the role of music education in contemporary American society. Participants at the Symposium agreed that music of a variety of styles and cultures should be included within school music curricula.[14] Interestingly, despite these ideas being over 50 years old, they remain sticking points in current conversations regarding the incorporation of popular music styles and practices into formal school music programs.

The *Music Educators Journal*, the primary journal of practicing American music teachers, devoted a section of their December 1979 issue to discuss the inclusion of popular music and rock in the music education curriculum. Topics addressed included bridging the gap between current popular music and school music practices, the issue of inappropriate lyrics, musical aspects of popular music, using popular music in the elementary classroom, and strategies for implementing popular music into the music education classroom. The *Journal* published additional special issues on popular music education again in 1991 and 2019.

In 2002, Music Educators National Conference (MENC) published *The Guide to Teaching with Popular Music.*[15] The guide included lesson plans and sheet music that were in line with the National Standards for Music Education as well as tips to help teachers get started using popular music in their instruction. Two years later, MENC published *Bridging the Gap: Popular Music and Music Education,*[16] which featured a collection of essays by well-known scholars and educators that addressed trends and issues related to the use of popular music in the classroom. PMP scholars and practitioners formed an Association for Popular Music Education (APME) in 2010 and later developed the *Journal of Popular Music Education* in 2017. National Association for Music Education (NAfME) established their own special research interest group (SRIG) for popular music in 2016 and authors published several popular music texts, including *The Routledge Research Companion to Popular Music Education* (2017) and *The Bloomsbury Handbook for Popular Music Education* (2019) to explore PMP-related themes. And in 2019, NAfME added an All-National Honors Modern Band as a part of their honor ensembles concerts, comprising some of the most talented high school popular musicians from across the United States.

Modern Approaches to Popular Music Pedagogies

While music educators and scholars have advocated for the inclusion of popular music styles and instrumentation for several decades, recent literature has explored the approaches and pedagogical techniques associated with these instruments and styles. Music educators cannot simply add popular music instruments and repertoire without changing the teacher-centered approach used in many music classrooms. To realize the full potential for popular music education in the classroom, music teachers need to transition from the role of director to the role of *facilitator*. According to music education scholar Radio Cremata, a facilitator "employs constructivist learning approaches through student-centered experiential processes."[17] In the role of a facilitator, the teacher is no longer the sole purveyor of instruction, directing all aspects of the rehearsal. In popular music ensembles, the facilitator instead responds to the needs of the students and takes cues from the group as to how and when the instructor is needed to provide direction. As a result, the music teacher must also negotiate when to inject themselves in the rehearsal process, and when to step back and allow students to collaboratively solve problems. Although directors of traditional music ensembles respond to the needs of their students as well, one difference is that the facilitator does not adhere to a set curriculum, nor do they always set out to achieve predetermined levels of progress each rehearsal. Classrooms that are teacher-facilitated may look and sound different from classrooms that are teacher-led. Facilitated classrooms may have stations for collaboration, students may be working on independent projects, there may be varied objectives and assessments depending on the learners' goals, and the teacher may be moving around the room instead of standing in front of the class. A facilitated classroom may be uncomfortable for teachers and learners who are accustomed to a teacher-led model, but this kind of environment leads to more creativity, collaboration, problem-solving, and other critical thinking skills essential to the notion of 21st-century education.

Music teachers of popular music ensembles may not be experts on every instrument and type of technology in a popular music classroom. This can be anxiety inducing or liberating, depending on the mindset of the educator. The music instructor must be willing to sit alongside the student as a co-learner in the music-making process.[18] The instructor becoming a learner is a very different role for the music teacher and one that must be addressed in music education preservice training, lest the next generation of music educators attempts to teach popular music without embracing aspects of PMP. Teachers may also assume the role of a producer in the classroom as described by scholar Clint Randles,

> to bring out what is good about the musician that is already there ... these types of teachers transcend tradition for the sake of their students' futures – that is, for this type of teacher, what lies ahead is more important than preserving the traditions that have gone before.[19]

In this role, the teacher recognizes and celebrates the skills students bring to the classroom instead of viewing them as empty vessels waiting to be filled with the knowledge of the all-knowing expert.

The approaches outlined in this book are not unique to popular music instruments. Indeed, student-centered approaches in traditional ensembles can include informal learning and nonformal teaching without five-line staff notation. Several scholars have written about opportunities for composing in choir[20], band and orchestra.[21] Musical Futures[22] has several online resources for bringing informal learning into traditional large ensemble spaces in addition to nonformal workshop ideas using Western classical music.

BENEFITS OF POPULAR MUSIC EDUCATION

American music educator and former MENC President Karl W. Gehrkens (1882–1975) coined the phrase "music for every child; every child for music," which later became the official slogan of the MENC, the predecessor to NAfME. "Music for every child; every child for music" is a great sentiment, but let us take a moment to think about what that means for music teachers. "Music for every child" has to mean every child, including those who don't want to play in traditional ensembles, those children who don't read music staff notation, those children who are interested in using technology to make their own music, children who want to pursue careers as rappers, and the countless other children whose musical preferences and identities are not currently being honored in traditional approaches to music education. If we as a community of music educators are going to embrace the belief of "music for every child; every child for music," then we need to immediately expand the instrumentation, repertoire, and pedagogical approaches we are using in the music classroom to provide access and opportunities for all learners.

As we imagine new approaches to music education, it is a useful exercise to think about what an ideal music education experience could be. In all schools, music would be available and relevant to all students, regardless of their abilities or musical preferences. The ideal music education space would honor the students' musical identities and would be a space where all music and instruments are welcome. An ideal music classroom would allow students to take risks without fear of failure and would focus on the musicality that the students already possess (asset model of education) rather than what they do not yet know (deficit model of education). We should recognize the best of our current practices when considering new approaches to teaching and learning. If the goal of music education is to democratize the space to include music that is meaningful to all students, we do not need to look any further than many of our elementary general music classrooms.[23] There are many elementary general music teachers who are writing songs with their students; incorporating ukulele, guitar, and technology in their lessons; using movement and dance; and teaching musical concepts through music that students know and love. The challenge sometimes lies in the transition from elementary general music classrooms to the traditional large ensembles in middle and high school. Once students enter these ensembles, they often stop composing, improvising, and moving, focusing instead on the reproduction of someone else's composition.

At the upper elementary and secondary levels, large ensembles such as band, choir, and orchestra represent a majority of the music offerings and are often viewed as the most participatory musical experiences. These ensembles have long-standing and important roles to play within a comprehensive program, but may also carry limitations that affect student participation in school music. While the traditional large ensemble experience attracts some students, nationally representative data demonstrate that 76 percent of students in the United States have not participated in a traditional ensemble at the secondary school level.[24] One reason for this lack of participation might be that while students, musical styles, and available technologies have changed drastically in the last 50 years, music education and preservice music teacher preparation largely has not.

Popular music ensembles and classes may serve as a complement to a large ensemble program, offering another participatory experience that broadens school music offerings instead of replacing them. Some PMPs may be transferred into large ensemble settings and the work of each might inform the other. Popular music experiences should not replace existing programs but instead provide additional benefits that enhance our school music programs. Scholars and teachers of popular music education have discovered several unique characteristics of programs that employ PMPs, leveraging the interest our students have for music that is typically found outside of school settings. These characteristics of democratic practice, cultural responsiveness, inclusivity (of levels and abilities), creativity and collaboration, and lifelong engagement are explored in the following sections.

Democratic Practice

In most school subjects, best practices include democratizing the space and encouraging students to take an active role in constructing their own knowledge through individual work, small group work, and as a class. In social studies classes, students demonstrate their understanding of topics by creating videos, building dioramas, or using tweets and social media posts to describe important moments in history. In English classes, students are often given opportunities for creative writing and are encouraged to add their own interpretations of classic works. Most proponents of PMPs recognize the educational benefits of a democratic approach to music teaching and learning, whereby students and teachers work together to construct knowledge that leads to new understandings. Students in a democratic classroom are provided ownership of their learning. Lisa DeLorenzo, a music education scholar, identified the following principles of democracy in a music classroom: shared decision-making, equal learning opportunities, acknowledgment of social contexts, and critical thinking.[25] We will apply these principles to a variety of activities and assessments throughout this textbook.

Culturally Responsive Pedagogy

To be truly democratic, classroom activities must be informed by the culture and perspective of all learners. As the racial and ethnic composition of our student population is ever-increasingly diverse, it is imperative that we critically examine the association between school music and a Western European (i.e., white) classical tradition. Past scholars have written about the "missing faces" in professional and school ensembles,[26] and your own experiences at honor festivals, All-State conferences – and perhaps, your local K-12 school music program – may confirm that our ensembles are disproportionately serving white and more affluent student populations.[27] We cannot be satisfied with this status quo, as educators are responsible for ensuring the well-being and success of every child in our classroom and caring about their growth as humans and individuals. Music education scholars Randall Allsup and Eric Shieh remind us "at the heart of teaching others is the moral imperative to care. Social justice education begins with adopting a disposition to perceive and then act against indecencies and injustices."[28] If we truly care for our students, those inside and outside of our classroom, then we must identify and raise awareness of oppressive acts against them.

In music education, this relates to access to school music programs, the financial cost of participating, and the ways we affirm or marginalize students through the content and delivery of our instruction. Through PMP practices, such as original songwriting and live performances, students may be able to promote social change and offer a "critical narrative of society."[29] By including a variety of musical styles, differentiating modes of learning, and recognizing contributions of a diverse body of performers, songwriters, and producers, we may attract a greater diversity of students to our school music programs. Not surprisingly, PMPs seem to connect with learners across all races, ethnicities, and socioeconomic backgrounds, as the learners themselves make choices regarding repertoire, style, and instrumentation. Popular music education is not a one-size-fits-all approach, and it functions to serve and affirm our students and their individual and collective cultures.

Inclusion

Music has the power to bring people together. Progressive school music programs are on the rise with an increasing number of programs offering nontraditional ensemble experiences such as mariachi, iPad ensembles, and drumming groups (bucket, world music, etc.). While compulsory elementary general music is inclusive by its nature (i.e., it serves all students), secondary school music education is not as inclusive as it could be. Take a concert band for example; most students can only participate in a high school concert band if they play a traditional band instrument and read traditional five-line staff notation. In many settings, students can only play in a high school band or orchestra if they started an ensemble appropriate instrument, such as trumpet or violin, in elementary or middle school. If students decide they would like to participate later, they may have missed their opportunity. What if they play electric guitar or piano? These instruments, while popular in society, do not have a place in most traditional ensembles outside of jazz band.

Several music education scholars have identified economic factors as a barrier to participation.[30] In many schools, students are responsible for renting or buying their own instruments. For students to be successful in these ensembles, it is often recommended that they take private lessons, pay for trips, and sacrifice work hours for evening rehearsals and weekend competitions. This precludes some students from having weekend jobs that might bring in necessary funds for their family. These financial considerations are often barriers to participation for students who might otherwise wish to participate in school instrumental ensembles. In contrast, PMPs celebrate our unique differences in skills and abilities as individuals instead of requiring us to assimilate to a common ideal or standard. Many school popular music ensembles and classes focus on the process rather than the product and are designed to maximize individual student growth rather than achieve high ensemble ratings. One of the measurements of success in a popular music program is its ability to engage individual students in creative music-making experiences, however possible. There is no single pathway, set instrumentation, or preapproved repertoire lists in PMPs, and all facets of the program may be adjusted to allow for participation at every level and ability.

Creativity and Collaboration

When you reflect on your own K-12 school music education, consider the balance of creative versus recreative learning experiences that were a part of your program. Chances are, you had many opportunities to perform the compositions and arrangements of others and very few (if any) opportunities to create original music. This imbalance does not align with the National Core Arts Standards, which promote *creating* music as an artistic process that should guide our standards and objectives in a variety of music classroom spaces. In high school visual arts classes, students learn about the great artists in history and they learn the techniques that these artists used to create their works. And why do they learn these techniques? So that students can create *their own* works of art. The focus of visual arts classes is for students to create new, original pieces. Can you imagine a visual arts class in high school that only focused on replicating paintings and sculptures created by other artists? Students in popular music ensembles and classes may have a unique opportunity to generate original music through songwriting, beat-making, lyric writing, and other creative processes. While some popular musicians perform masterworks by other artists, they largely work as individuals or in groups to develop and share original musical ideas.

All ensembles, regardless of style, are inherently collaborative. However, popular music engages students in unique collaborations that imitate partnerships found in the professional music industry among songwriters, performers, producers, audio engineers, and promoters. Popular music classes may engage students in collaborative project-based learning activities in which students assume these professional roles and work together toward creating a product (e.g., music video or album). These collaborations may occur within a classroom or between multiple classrooms or even school buildings. Through multitrack recording (discussed in Part II of this textbook), teachers may combine the performances of elementary, middle school, and high school students from around the district. One group of students could record the lyrics to a song while another group records the chorus. Students in a music technology class might write an original song that includes the school's band, orchestra, or chorus. Teachers can take collaborations a step further by creating partnerships with other schools, community members, and professionals in the industry. There is no limit to the size and scope of collaborations in a school's popular music program. Through PMPs, teachers can facilitate collaborations that stretch the classroom walls and develop relationships with musicians everywhere.

Lifelong Engagement

Music in society is made in a variety of places including bars, basements, garages, places of worship, around campfires, and on personal technology devices such as the iPad. Think about the ways that you see adults engaging in live music; these musical experiences probably include karaoke, open mic nights, and cover bands. For the last century, the two best-selling instruments in the United States have been the guitar and keyboard. And as more and more individuals are making music using smartphones and iPads,[31] school music programs will need to include portable technologies to remain relevant. While music education spaces do not need to solely include the musical instruments that society uses to engage in music-making, to ignore them completely seems to be at odds with the profession's desire to promote lifelong music-makers.

MOVING FORWARD

This is an exciting time to embark on a career in music education. PMPs have finally gained momentum and acceptance in the field, and the response from K-12 students participating in popular music ensembles is overwhelmingly positive. Through PMPs, music teachers are involving more students in our school music programs, which are in turn looking more representative of our overall population in terms of race, gender, socioeconomic status, and musical preference. If we as music educators can agree that "music for every child; every child for music" means that all students have the right to a music education that develops their talents and abilities in a way that prepares them for lifelong music-making, then we need to expand our practices. We must allow these changes to complicate our professional lives. These changes will include which types of music, instruments, and approaches are welcome, and will challenge us to meaningfully consider which students are excluded from current music education practices and how we as music educators are complicit in forming barriers to participation for marginalized groups. These changes will take some effort. However, as scholar Wayne Bowman puts it, "the effort required to keep things as they are will surpass the effort change entails."[32] As a music teacher (or future music teacher), you have a tremendous opportunity to make a difference in the lives of your students and in your communities. PMPs can be transformative and life-changing, especially for students who have had limited access to school music in the past. By engaging with PMPs you will be a part of a growing population of educators blazing a trail for music education in the 21st century. We hope you enjoy the journey.

Takeaways

- Both "traditional" and "emerging" musical practices have strengths that complement one another in a school music program.
- There is not one singular pedagogy to teaching popular music.
- Scholars have written about the importance of popular music education for a century, and many conferences, journals, and textbooks have examined ways to implement popular music in schools.
- Many modern approaches to teaching popular music encourage a constructivist learning environment.

Discussion Questions

1. What would your ideal school music classroom look like? What kind of popular music opportunities might it include, if any?
2. Do you believe that popular music has merit as an academic pursuit? Does it belong in school?

3. Is there a place for popular music in all or just some music classes?
4. Can you identify students you went to school with who may have benefited from popular music offerings? How do you think these opportunities would have changed their perceptions of school music?
5. What are potential obstacles to implementing a popular music class or ensemble in schools? What are possible solutions to these obstacles?

Notes

1 Woody, "Popular Music in School," 32.
2 Kratus, "Music Education at the Tipping Point," 42–48.
3 Woody, "Popular Music in School," 32–37.
4 Key terms in bold font are defined in the glossary.
5 Bowman, "Taking Popular Music Seriously," 29–49.
6 Allsup, "Another Perspective: Our 'Both/And' Moment," 85.
7 Green, *Music Education as Critical Theory and Practice*.
8 Weston, "Place of Practice in Tertiary Popular Music Studies," 101–16.
9 Rodriguez, *Popular Music and Music Education*.
10 Green, "Popular Music Education in and for Itself," 101–18.
11 Musical Futures Australia, "Learning and Playing Music in the Classroom."
12 For a more complete history of the inclusion of popular music in United States school music programs, see Powell (in press) A History of Popular Music Education and Modern Band in United States K-12 Music Education, *Journal of Historical Research in Music Education*.
13 Choate, *Report of Tanglewood Symposium*.
14 Ibid.
15 Schmid and March, "Guide to Teaching with Popular Music."
16 Rodriguez, *Popular Music and Music Education*.
17 Cremata, "Facilitation in Popular Music Education," 63–82.
18 Green, *How Popular Musicians Learn*.
19 Randles, "Music Teacher as Writer and Producer," 36–52.
20 Kerchner and Strand, *Composing in Choir*.
21 Randles and Stringham, *Composing in Band and Orchestra*.
22 Musical Futures, www.musicalfutures.org.
23 Olesko, "Reconciling Authority and Autonomy."
24 Elpus and Abril, "Who Enrolls in School Music?"
25 DeLorenzo, *Giving Voice to Democracy*.
26 DeLorenzo, "Missing Faces from Orchestra," 39–46.
27 Elpus and Abril, "High School Music Ensemble Students," 128–45; and Elpus and Abril, "Who Enrolls in School Music?"
28 Allsup and Shieh, "Social Justice and Music Education," 47–51.
29 Woodward, "Social Justice and Popular Music Education," 395–411.
30 Corenblum and Marshall, "Predicting Students' Intentions to Continue Studying Music," 128–40; Culp and Clauhs, "Factors that Affect Participation in Secondary School Music" (in press); Elpus and Abril, "High School Music Ensemble Students," 128–45; Kinney, "Selected Nonmusic Predictors of Urban Students' Decisions to Enroll and Persist in Middle School Band Programs,"

334–50; Klinedust, "Predicting Performance Achievement and Retention of Fifth-Grade Instrumental Students," 225–38; and McCarthy, "Individualized Instruction, Student Achievement, and Dropout in an Urban Elementary Instrumental Music Program," 59–69.

31 Randles, "Disruptive Performance Technologies," 431–40.

32 Bowman, "Taking Popular Music Seriously," 29–49.

PART I

Instrument Techniques

OBJECTIVES

- **Compare** instruments typically found in popular music settings.
- **Demonstrate** proficiency on popular music instruments.
- **Discuss** strategies for differentiation using popular music instruments.
- **Describe** the role of individual instruments in an ensemble.
- **Connect** the philosophical foundations of popular music education to instrument pedagogy.
- **Explain** the function of iconic notation including chord diagrams and tablature in a popular music setting.

Introduction to Guitar, Bass, and Ukulele

This chapter introduces forms of notation and instrument techniques that are shared among the guitar, electric bass, and ukulele. It provides an overview of iconic notation systems that are commonly used in popular music classrooms, including chord diagrams, chord charts, tablature, and strumming pattern images, as well as instructional approaches and opportunities for differentiation on fretted instruments. This chapter serves as an introduction to fretted instruments, with additional techniques and approaches specific to the guitar, electric bass, and ukulele presented later in the book. We highly recommend reading this introductory chapter before the specific instrument chapters, especially if you have limited experience with playing or teaching fretted instruments.

Frets are the defining characteristic of a fretted instrument. They are raised metal or plastic strips that separate an instrument into intervals. When pressing down on the fretboard while playing, the raised frets change the length of the vibrating string, impacting the pitch. While it is typical for a teacher to say "put your finger on the third fret," this is not actually where the finger should be placed on an instrument. The finger, in this example, would really go in between the second and third fret, but not *on* the third fret. It may be helpful to initially identify this place as a box, since the space between the frets is in the shape of a rectangle. This instruction will be clearer to students and will prevent them from developing poor technique. Once students are comfortable placing their fingers in the correct spot, you can refer to this placement as the "third fret" instead of the "third box" (Figure 2.1).

◥ FRETTED INSTRUMENT TIP

Students should place their fretting finger close to the fret, but not on the fret, for the best possible sound.

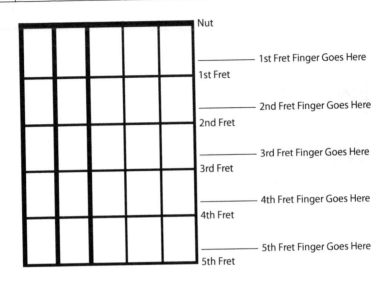

FIGURE 2.1
Guitar Fretboard

NOTATION FOR GUITAR, BASS, AND UKULELE

As the presence of popular music continues to expand in K-12 classrooms across the United States, it is important for educators to consider the forms of notation used to introduce fretted instruments and repertoire to their students. Guitar, electric bass and ukulele are instruments with deep cultural roots, traditions, and practices. Educators bringing them into the classroom should be aware of these practices to avoid creating a "school version" of engagement with these instruments. There are method books for guitar, electric bass, and ukulele that look similar to those for violin, flute, and saxophone – and may even be part of the same method book series – but these resources might not be the most appropriate choices for classrooms engaging with popular music, as many popular musicians learn by ear and with the aid of iconic notation. While music educators may think of notation as synonymous with a five-line staff, NAfME defines notation more broadly as "a visual representation of musical sounds" in the National Core Arts Music Standards Glossary.[1] NAfME elaborates to define **iconic notation** as a "representation of sound and its treatment using lines, drawings, pictures."[2] Players of fretted instruments in popular music settings often rely heavily on iconic notation in the form of chord diagrams, chord charts, tablature, and strumming pattern images. After learning how to decode different forms of iconic notation, students can use diagrams, chord charts, and lead sheets to perform melodies, rhythms, chords, and complete songs. To begin reading notation for fretted instruments, it is important to first understand how the fingers are numbered. Specific fingerings are not always assigned to each chord, especially as musicians develop proficiency on the instruments and make musical decisions based on chord

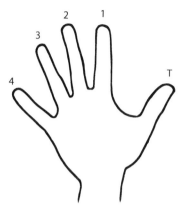

FIGURE 2.2
Finger Numbers for Guitar, Ukulele, and Bass

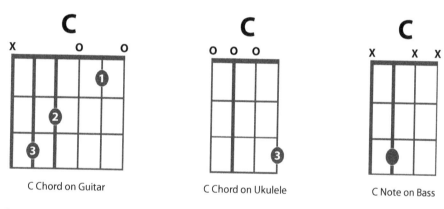

C Chord on Guitar   C Chord on Ukulele   C Note on Bass

FIGURE 2.3
Chord/Fretboard Diagrams for Guitar, Ukulele, and Bass

progressions. Unlike the piano, fingerings for guitar, ukulele, and bass start with the index finger as "1" instead of the thumb (Figure 2.2).

Figure 2.3 illustrates how chord diagrams match the fretboard of each instrument. The thick line at the top of the diagram represents the nut of instrument, which is the part of the neck that spaces out strings at the transition between the fingerboard and the tuners. The thickest (lowest pitched) strings are on the left of the diagram for the guitar and bass, and the ukulele strings are placed in order from left to right: G–C–E–A. Images of chord charts that you might find on the internet will often not have the thick line for the nut or thicker depictions of the lower-pitched strings; we have provided those here so that the chord diagrams are easier to understand. On right-handed guitars, basses, and ukuleles, the strings on the left side of the chord diagram are "closest to your nose" and strings on the right side of the diagram are "closest to your toes." The nose and toes landmarks are useful when helping others identify the strings on fretted instruments. The dots on each chord diagram indicate where to place the fingers on the fretboard, and finger numbers are often included in the middle of the dot. Please note that the numbers on a chord diagram refer to the fingers and not the number of the fret. Figure 2.3 illustrates the C major chord on the guitar and ukulele, and how to play a low C (sounding two octaves below middle C) on the electric bass.[3]

The "X" above the strings in Figure 2.3 indicates that the string is not to be played (strummed, plucked, or picked). Therefore, the lowest string would not be included in the C major chord notated above for guitar. The "O" above the strings in Figure 2.3 indicates that the string is played without pressing it down on any frets (i.e., an open string). Three of the four ukulele strings are played this way for the C major chord notated above.

A **capo** is a device used to hold down the strings across a fret, replicating the function of the nut. By placing the capo across the strings, you are shortening the length of the vibrating strings, thus raising the pitch. Placing the capo across the first fret will raise the strings under the capo by a half step. So, if you place the capo across the first fret and play an Emi shape, the chord will sound as an Fmi chord. If you place the capo on the second fret and play the Emi shape, the chord will sound as F♯mi. Using a capo allows you to play songs in more difficult keys using easier chord shapes. For example, if a song is in the key of G♯, you can simply place a capo on the first fret and play a G chord. The capo across the first fret will raise the pitches of the G chord a half step to G♯. Visit http://popmusicped.com for a videothe pitchesnstthen of the capo.

Tablature

Tablature (or tab, for short) is a system of music notation which indicates the string and fret that should be played. Tab is one of the main forms of notation for guitar, bass, and string players. This form of notation dates back hundreds of years and is identified as one form of standard notation by the National Core Arts Standards.[4] Guitar tab has six lines representing the six strings of the instrument (E–A–D–G–B–E). Bass and ukulele tablature most often have four lines representing the four strings of the instrument (Figure 2.4).

Tablature may seem to be written upside down, but if you were to look down at a fretted instrument, this is the order of the strings that you would see.

Figure 2.5 illustrates how an A minor pentatonic scale would be notated for guitar using both tablature and five-line staff notation. The

FIGURE 2.4
Headstocks and Matching Tablature for Guitar (top), Bass (middle), and Ukulele (bottom)

FIGURE 2.5
Guitar Tablature for an A Minor Pentatonic Scale

numbers on each line (string) indicate which fret box to press. Note that tablature does not indicate which finger to use in the fret box. Since it is difficult to accurately express rhythms in this form of notation, tablature works best when learning familiar songs. There are some rhythm notation systems used with tab which indicate the division of beats or use stems, flags, and dots to indicate rhythms.

> Several popular music learning apps (e.g., Yousician, Rocksmith) combine tablature with a color-coding system for fingerings, rectangles that represent note lengths, and a bouncing ball to help the player perform the tablature accurately and in time with a recording. See Chapter 12 for a more complete description of tablature-based assessment tools.

Chord Chart

A **chord chart** provides a fretted instrument player with information about the chord progression and form of a song (Figure 2.6). Chord charts may include **slash notation** to illustrate the meter (how many beats are in a measure) and harmonic rhythm (one chord per measure versus two chords per measure). Specific strumming patterns may not be included in a chord chart and players are free to improvise their own rhythms (also known as **comping,** an abbreviation for accompaniment) when playing chords or a **bass line.**

> There are many resources online for free chord charts for guitar, ukulele, and electric bass. Visit http://jamzone.littlekidsrock.org for free PowerPoint files to build your own chord charts.

FIGURE 2.6
Chord Chart Excerpt with Chord Diagrams and Slash Notation

Lead Sheet

In **lead sheet** notation, a melody is written on a five-line staff with chord symbols expressed above each measure. In Figure 2.7 below, the lead sheet provides the melody, lyrics, and chord progression to the opening line of "Happy Birthday." The fretted instrument player can then incorporate the chords or create a bass line as desired. Lead sheet notation is typically found in fake books, which are used in jam sessions and gigs by many jazz, Latin, and contemporary musicians. Fake books provide a canon of repertoire for musicians who may not regularly work together to easily form ensembles and perform as a group.

FRETTED INSTRUMENT TECHNIQUES

Barre Chords

When playing a **barre chord** (sometimes spelled "bar") on a guitar or ukulele, one finger presses down multiple strings across a single fret. Barring the strings replicates the function of the nut at a desired location on the instrument. As the first finger holds down the strings across a given fret, the other three fingers are free to play chord shapes on the fretboard. In Figure 2.8, the chord diagram on the left demonstrates open strings (where the nut acts like a "zero" barre) and the chord diagram on the right represents a full barre, using the full first finger at the 2nd fret. Barre chords are useful for the guitar and ukulele (and sometimes bass) as they allow a player to use the same hand position to perform chords in multiple keys, simply by moving the barre chord shape up

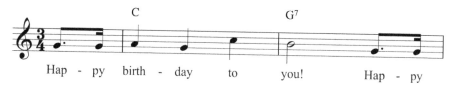

FIGURE 2.7
Lead Sheet Notation for "Happy Birthday"

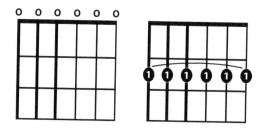

FIGURE 2.8
Open Strings versus Full Barre at the 2nd Fret

and down the fretboard. In other words, the hand position for F major, G, major, G♭ major, and A♭, major could be the same shape used on the 1st, 2nd, 3rd, and 4th frets, respectively. More details about specific barre chord shapes for the guitar and ukulele are provided in Chapters 3 and 5.

> When playing barre chords, the finger is like a movable capo and can be placed anywhere on the fretboard.

Strumming Patterns

Strumming patterns are repeating rhythms used to strum the strings of a fretted instrument. They are often written down as visual representations of the rhythm and motion of the hand, with indications of when the instrument is played. Two common strumming pattern diagrams include (1) a system that uses arrows to indicate the direction of the strum, and (2) a counting system that represents the rhythm of the strum using numbers and plus signs. Often, beginners start by strumming down on the beat (downstroke), and strum up on the division of the beat, or off beat (upstroke). In the arrow-based system of strumming patterns, the downstrokes are represented by black downward-facing arrows, and the upstrokes are represented by gray upward-facing arrows. In Figure 2.9, the player would strum down on each of the beats, represented here using both notation systems for strumming patterns.

The strumming pattern in Figure 2.10 should be performed by playing a downstroke on the beat and an upstroke on the off beat.

If the arrow is missing, or the number is grayed out, simply skip over the strings as you strum (Figure 2.11). Once students understand how this works, they can create their own strumming patterns and write out the corresponding

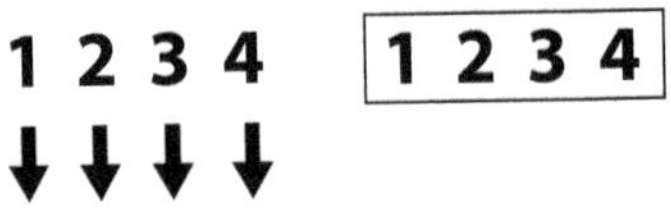

1 2 3 4   **1 2 3 4**
↓ ↓ ↓ ↓

FIGURE 2.9
Strumming Pattern that Emphasizes the Beats

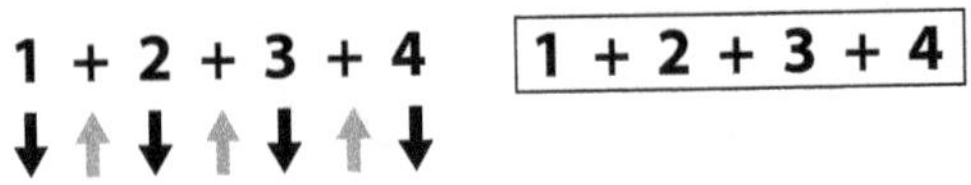

1 + 2 + 3 + 4   **1 + 2 + 3 + 4**
↓ ↑ ↓ ↑ ↓ ↑ ↓

FIGURE 2.10
Strumming Pattern that Emphasizes Beats and Off Beat

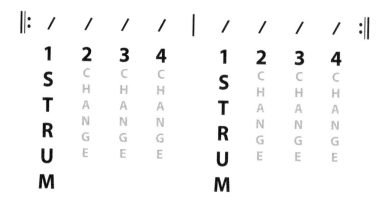

FIGURE 2.11
Syncopated Strumming Pattern

‖: /   /   /   / | /   /   /   /   :‖

1	**2**	**3**	**4**	**1**	**2**	**3**	**4**
S	C	C	C	**S**	C	C	C
T	H	H	H	**T**	H	H	H
R	A	A	A	**R**	A	A	A
U	N	N	N	**U**	N	N	N
M	G	G	G	**M**	G	G	G
	E	E	E		E	E	E

FIGURE 2.12
Taking Time to Change Chords
Image courtesy of Little Kids Rock

rhythmic notation. You can also start by having students create their own strumming patterns before introducing strum pattern notation.

Changing Between Chords

There are several pedagogical strategies that help students be successful when changing chords on a fretted instrument. These approaches will allow students to experience success more easily and progress more quickly.

Divide Up the Chords

Instead of asking students to switch back and forth between two different chords, you can have half of the class play one chord, and the other half play the other chord. Since the students will only be responsible for playing one chord, they are more likely to experience success than if they had to switch between chords.

Allow More Time to Make the Change

Students can play a chord on the first beat of the measure, and then use beats 2, 3, and 4 to change to the next chord, as shown in Figure 2.12. Do not worry about the strumming pattern until students feel comfortable changing between chords.

Slow Down!

Another useful strategy is to slow down the tempo so that students do not feel rushed when changing chords. YouTube, Audacity, and the Amazing Slow Downer are all tools that allow the user to adjust the tempo of a recording. The playback speed of a YouTube video is found in the settings of the video player. It is a built-in feature that allows any video to be performed at various speeds in increments of 5 percent. For a "how to" video for these technologies, visit http://popmusicped.com.

Economy of Motion

Instead of taking the hand away from the fretboard and then placing fingers back on the strings, find pivot fingers that allow the hand to move as little as possible. For example, when switching between the C and Ami chords on the guitar, you can see that the first and second fingers stay in the same place (Figure 2.13). You only need to move the third finger to change between the chords.

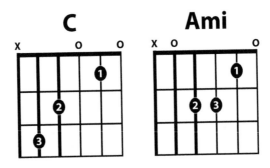

FIGURE 2.13
Pivoting on the 2nd Finger when Changing from C to A minor

DIFFERENTIATION

There are many opportunities for differentiation using fretted instruments. This differentiation can take the form of using different types of notation or simplifying more difficult chords or rhythms to make them more accessible to all students. When playing guitar or ukulele, students can use fewer strings to play easier versions of chords. Students with less experience can use power chords and three-string chords as alternatives to more complex chords. For examples of these chords, please refer to Chapter 3: Guitar and Chapter 5: Ukulele. By combining easier versions of chords and simplified strumming patterns, guitar and ukulele students of widely different ability and experience levels can perform together in the same space. Here is one simple example of how students can choose their parts depending on their comfort level with playing the instrument. Students can also choose techniques from multiple levels if for example, they can play the full G chord but only feel comfortable playing on the first downbeat of each measure. Remember, student choice is a crucial element of popular music and a music pedagogies teacher should resist "assigning" parts to students based on the teacher's perception of their skill levels.

Beginning Group

- Play an "Easy G" chord.
- Strum on the first downbeat of each measure.

Intermediate Group

- Play a full G chord.
- Strum on every downbeat.

Advanced Group

- Play a G major barre chord.
- Strumming pattern with syncopation or create their own.

Another approach to differentiation is to provide the bass line, chord diagrams (of varying levels), and pentatonic scale to any combination of guitar, bass, and ukulele players. The students could determine which is most comfortable for them and perform it alongside the other parts. As the chord progression repeats, students could practice more challenging parts, moving from playing root notes to easy/medium/advanced chords, and eventually improvising with a pentatonic scale. The bass players could switch between performing the chord roots (bass line), creating a **walking bass line**, and improvising while the other fretted instruments provided a harmonic accompaniment.

CONCLUSION

Guitars, basses, and ukuleles have provided amateur and professional musicians with melodic and harmonic tools for centuries and are increasingly common in American K-12 school music programs. Music teachers must be familiar with the basic techniques, approaches, and forms of notation used when introducing these instruments in school. The reader should take some time to become familiar with the chord diagrams, tablature, and strumming patterns presented here before reading the individual chapters on guitar, bass, and ukulele. Avoid the temptation to teach these instruments just as you would teach traditional band and orchestra instruments, and try to embrace the spirit of popular music: learning by ear, building a repertoire of songs, and jamming with friends as you learn these instruments. Outside of school settings, most beginning popular musicians first learn chords to play songs that are meaningful to them. Connecting instruction with the students' musical interests is an important element of popular music education. Finally, be sure to explore all the fretted instruments, as being a multi-instrumentalist is an important characteristic of a popular musician and popular music educator.

Takeaways

- Iconic notation, in the form of chord diagrams, chord charts, tablature, and strumming pattern images, is commonly used when introducing fretted instruments in a popular music setting.
- A barre chord allows ukulele and guitar players to create a movable capo, unlocking multiple chords of the same quality using a consistent hand position on different frets of the instrument.
- Playing simplified chords, taking time in between chords, and slowing down the tempo are techniques to help less experienced players have early success on a fretted instrument.
- Fretted instruments allow for differentiation as players of varying abilities can perform multiple parts simultaneously as a group in class.

Discussion Questions

1. What is your personal experience with playing fretted instruments?
2. How do forms of iconic notation help or hinder musical development?
3. Which fretted instrument would you introduce to a class first, and why?
4. How is standard notation for these fretted instruments (e.g., tablature, chord charts) similar to and different from traditional five-line staff notation?
5. How might you be able to incorporate aural skills and playing by ear into the classroom using the fretted instruments discussed in this chapter?

Notes

1 NAfME, "Core Music Standards Glossary."
2 Ibid.
3 The electric bass sounds one octave lower than it is written in five-line staff notation. While this low C would sound two octaves below middle C, it would be notated one octave below middle C.
4 Ibid.

Guitar

If you have not yet reviewed Chapter 2: Introduction to Guitar, Bass, and Ukulele, please do so before continuing with this chapter.

M any students are immediately drawn to the guitar. The instrument, the musicians who play it, and the music it creates, all capture the imagination. It's no surprise the guitar has been one of the most popular instruments sold in North America over the last 50 years;[1] its inclusion in a school music program can provide students with the opportunity to play music from a diverse array of genres and the skills needed to engage in lifelong music-making. This chapter presents approaches designed to get students up and strumming as quickly as possible, initially using simplified chords so they can play the music that they know and love from day one. This chapter starts with simplified three-string chords that only require no more than one finger to play. These chords allow students to experience immediate success and will get them playing songs they recognize much more quickly. This chapter also introduces the concepts of tablature, **power chords**, and barre chords, as well as pedagogical tips for teaching the guitar.

BASICS

This section provides some technical information that will be helpful to you as a teacher, but is not necessary for students to learn until they have already experienced some success playing the instrument. This includes the parts of the guitar (Figure 3.1) as well as steps for tuning the instrument. Eventually, students should know this information, but we recommend that classes start playing right away and learn theory and the technical concepts of the guitar later as it becomes necessary. It is tempting to start the first guitar class by reviewing the parts of the guitar, names of the strings, and other theory-based concepts, but students won't retain this information as quickly if it is not relevant to their success. While you will need to model how to hold the guitar

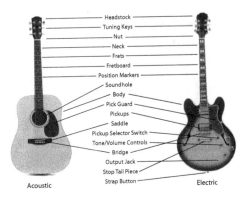

FIGURE 3.1
Parts of the Guitar

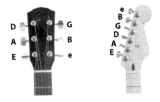

FIGURE 3.2
Tuning Keys/Pegs with Corresponding String Names

and **pick**, students will be much more receptive to learning about the parts of the guitar and the names of the guitar strings once they have played chords and familiar songs. If the guitars are in tune, students can play simple chords and songs without knowing the names of the guitar strings. Start with playing songs as soon as possible, and your students will be hooked!

Tuning the guitar

New strings will continue to stretch for a while after they are put on the guitar, causing the instrument to go out of tune. Once the guitar strings are broken in, they should be able to hold their tuning without students (or you) needing to adjust the **tuning keys** (or tuning pegs) too often (Figure 3.2). We recommend checking the tuning of each guitar with a tuner before each playing session.

Students can identify the order of the guitar strings through an acronym. Two popular sentences to help beginners remember the strings are:

Eddie Ate Dynamite, Good Bye Eddie
Elephants And Donkeys Grow Big Ears

FIGURE 3.3
Guitar Strap Buttons

The first part of these sentences also works for the order of the four strings on the electric bass (Chapter 4), E, A, D, G: Eddie Ate Dynamite ... Good; and Elephants And Donkeys Grow. Students can also create their own acronym: E____ A____ D____ G____ B____ E____.

Holding the Guitar

The guitar can be held while sitting down or standing up with the help of a guitar strap (see Figure 3.4). A right-handed guitar is held by the neck with the left hand, resting the body of the guitar on the lap. The indentation on the body of the guitar will rest on the right leg. Classical guitarists often rest the guitar on their laps with with the headstock raised close to a 45 degree angle; this is a stylistic preference and students should choose the playing position that is most comfortable for them. Students will need guitar straps if they stand while playing their instruments. If a guitar does not have strap buttons (Figure 3.3), these can be purchased inexpensively at most music stores or online.

◣ RIGHT-HANDED OR LEFT-HANDED?

The choice to accommodate left-handed students with a left-handed guitar often depends on a few factors, including the availability of left-handed guitars in the classroom and students' prior experience playing a left-handed guitar. If students already have some experience playing a left-handed guitar before coming into your class, then switching them to a right-handed guitar will likely be detrimental to their progress. If new to playing the instrument, left-handed students can be successful playing a right-handed guitar. A useful analogy for encouraging left-handed students to play a right-handed guitar is to look at the piano; there is not a left-handed version of the piano. We all learn to play the piano the same way, regardless of which hand is dominant. This is also true for the string instruments of the orchestra and all the wind instruments in the concert band. Depending on the type of guitars that you have in the classroom, some of them can simply be strung "backwards" with strings in reverse order to accommodate left-handed players. Some slight alterations to the bridge and the nut might be necessary. Teachers will also need to provide reversed chord chart diagrams for left-handed students because traditional chord chart diagrams will be backwards for them.

Holding a Pick

Most popular music styles require the use of a guitar pick and we highly recommend introducing the pick at the start of instruction. While you can use your thumb and index finger to play or strum guitar strings, this is likely going to result in sore fingers, especially when using steel-string guitars. Picks come in many thicknesses, but a medium pick (between 0.70–0.84 mm) is good for beginners. Thinner picks work best for strumming while thicker picks are ideal for playing single note melody lines on the guitar. The pick should be held between the thumb and index finger so that the tip extends beyond the finger (Figure 3.5). It may be helpful to imagine the hand and pick creating the shape of a chicken, with the pick (beak) protruding from the hand (face of the chicken). Tightly squeezing the pick can cause the hand to cramp, while

FIGURE 3.4
Sitting and Standing with the Guitar

FIGURE 3.5
Holding a Pick

holding it too loosely will cause it to fly out of the hand or drop into the sound hole. A firm grip in between those extremes will work best.

Strumming

The strumming hand and arm should be relaxed as students strum the strings. If students display tension as they strum, they should be encouraged to stop, relax, and start over. The wrist and elbow should move together to create a natural motion. Instruct students to avoid locking the wrist if it appears they are only moving their arm at the elbow joint. Students can begin to practice strumming by muting the strings with the left hand and strumming the strings with a pick in the right hand. This creates a percussive sound, which works well in echo pattern activities. By muting the strings, students can focus on their strumming technique without worrying about fingering chords with the left hand.

> Visit popmusicped.com for video examples and explanations of basic guitar techniques.

APPROACHES

Begin with Simplified Chords

Depending on the method of instruction, students may initially find it challenging to play chord progressions of their favorite songs. Fortunately, **simplified chords** enable beginners to have instant success as they learn the instrument and these chords accommodate students of varying abilities and skill sets. Figure 3.6 presents a variety of ways (from simple to complex) to play a G chord on the guitar. The first option only requires students to play the three highest pitched strings. This three-string chord is going to be easier for

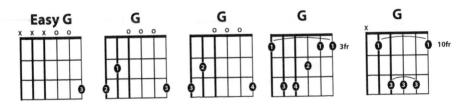

FIGURE 3.6
Easy, Medium, and Advanced Versions of the G Major Chord

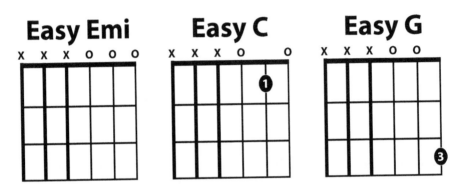

FIGURE 3.7
Three-String Chords

beginning students to master right away. Every triad can be performed using the top three strings of the guitar, so there is a simplified version of almost every chord commonly used in popular music.

> By folding a paper towel and sliding it under the three thickest strings (Low E, A, D), students can concentrate on the fingering for simplified chords without worrying about accidentally playing unwanted strings. A modified version of the guitar, made by Loog, includes only the three highest pitched strings (G, B, High E). This instrument may be useful for accommodating students with special needs, or as an introduction to the guitar. Visit https://loogguitars.com/ for more information.

Once students understand how chord diagrams work, they can easily learn a few simplified chords and start playing songs right away. Figure 3.7 shows three simplified three-string chords that may be used to perform hundreds of songs. Remember, an "X" above the chord diagram indicates that the string is not to be played. So, for each three-string chord pictured in Figure 3.7, the three thickest, lowest pitched strings (E, A, D) are not played. The three thinnest, highest pitched strings (G, B, High E) are played.

Three-String Chord Activities

Echo Patterns
Once students can play these three simple chords, there are several activities they can do to build confidence in playing familiar chords. One common approach is an echo pattern activity in which the teacher (or a student leader) plays a four-beat strumming pattern using one of the chords and the class repeats this pattern. Adding a simple drum beat play-along track to this activity can help students keep a steady beat while they strum, and it makes the activity more engaging because everyone likes to play along with a drummer. And since a drum beat play-along is not in any specific key, you can use the same play-along to introduce or review any chord or chord progression.

Playing Familiar Songs
Once the three simplified chords are mastered, there are hundreds of songs that can easily be played on the guitar. Many songs have sections that use only the I and the V chords, which can be played with C and G chords, respectively. By reversing the order and playing G to C we have unlocked songs that alternate between I and IV chords. It is not necessary to play the entire song, as students will be excited to play sections of songs they know. For a list of songs that use the chords G, C, and Emi (or the I, IV, and vi chords), check out Little Kids Rock's *Jam Zone,* www.chordify.net, ultimate-guitar.com, or any number of online guitar music sites.

Play-Alongs
Play-along videos are a great way to engage students with familiar songs. Most play-along videos contain the chords and lyrics of the music with the chord to be played highlighted at the appropriate time with the audio track. There are hundreds of free play-along videos on YouTube, and it is easy to make your own play-along video using PowerPoint and a movie editor such as iMovie or Windows Movie Maker. For play-along video resources, check out http://popmusicped.com.

IMPROVISATION AND COMPOSITION

Lessons in improvisation and composition can begin right away. As soon as students can play a chord, they can write a song; and as soon as students can play a note, they can improvise. Chapter 13 of this book includes beginning strategies for songwriting, improvising, and arranging.

Learning Full Chords
After practicing simplified chords and gaining experience with reading chord diagrams, students will be ready to learn full chords on the guitar. We recommend starting with **open chords**, in which one or more of the strings are played

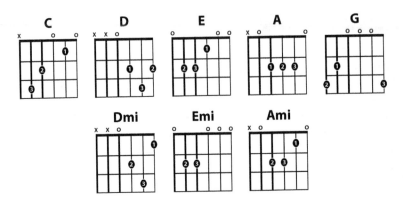

FIGURE 3.8
Frequently Used Open Chords

open (without being fretted). These chords are easier for beginners, because not all the strings are held down with the fretting hand. Figure 3.8 presents some of the most frequently used open chords.

When introducing full chords to students, have them place their fingers on the strings one at a time. Once they have all the fingers in place, they should gently squeeze them down, using the thumb placed on the back of the neck to gently apply pressure. The position of the thumb will shift slightly for each chord. Students should play one string at a time to ensure none of the strings are muted or fuzzy. If a string does not sound, it is likely because it is being muted by another finger or the string is not pressed against the fretboard hard enough. For tips to help students practice changing between chords, review Chapter 2: Introduction to Fretted Instruments.

The Power of Power Chords

The most common power chords are two- or three-note chords featuring the root and 5th notes of a chord. These chords do not have major or minor qualities because they do not contain the 3rd. Power chords provide possibilities in the classroom because they are easy to play; by simply moving the power chord shape up and down the neck of the guitar, students can play an F♯5 chord as easily as a G5 chord (it is the same shape, just one fret away). Difficult chords (e.g., B, Bmi, C♯) become much easier to play, making virtually any song accessible for all students. Now that is some power!

Power chords can either start on the low E string or the A string. Figure 3.9 illustrates the placement of the first finger on the 3rd fret (indicated by 3fr) of the low E string and the third finger on the 5th fret of the A string. In this example, the index finger is on a G, therefore this is a G5 power chord. Figure 3.10 is an A5 power chord, which is played with the first finger on the 5th fret (indicated by 5fr) of the E string and the third finger on the 7th fret of the A string.

In Figure 3.11, we add the pinky finger to the D string which doubles the root at the octave. In a three-note power chord, this shape provides the root,

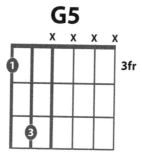

FIGURE 3.9
G5 Power Chord

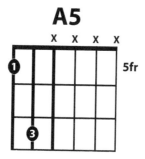

FIGURE 3.10
A5 Power Chord

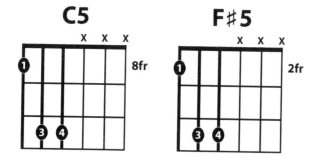

FIGURE 3.11
Three-Note Power Chords

5th, and upper octave root of the chord. Again, there is no 3rd, so this shape can be used to substitute for any major, minor, or dominant chord quality. One finger may also be used to play multiple strings. In Figure 3.12 the third finger frets two strings at the same time. This is called a **barre**.

G Power Chord

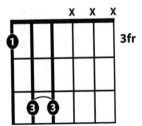

FIGURE 3.12
Barring with the Third Finger

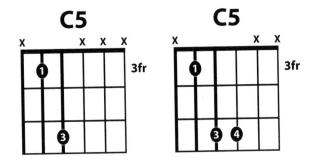

FIGURE 3.13
Power Chords Beginning on the A String

A power chord can also start on the A string, which is especially useful for chords such as B♭, B, C♯/D♭, and D♯/E♭. Figure 3.13 shows the two-string and three-string power chords for a C5 chord starting on the A string. Because a C is three half steps above A, the 3rd fret of the A string is a C.

The Benefit of Barre Chords

Barre chords expand upon the basic idea of power chords as a movable chord shape; finger presses down multiple strings across a single fret. Barring the strings turns your finger into a movable capo, replicating the function of the nut on the guitar. As a finger holds down the strings across a given fret, other fingers are available to play various chord shapes on the fretboard.

The more students practice playing barre chords, the more strength they will develop in their fingers. It does take time to become proficient at playing barre chords, so encourage your students to have patience and not become frustrated. So why are barre chords important? Much like power chords, barre chords make songs with difficult chord progressions more accessible. Chords with roots of A♯/B♭, B, C♯/D♭, D♯/E♭, F♯/G♭, and G♯/A♭ all require barres. And once barre chords are mastered, songs can easily be transposed into any key.

Because the same barre chord shape works for several chords, transposing a song from G major to either F♯ major or A♭ major is a breeze.

> Visit http://popmusicped.com for a video tutorial on power chords and barre chords.

The examples shown here demonstrate how the shape of the E major chord becomes a barre shape to play F major and F♯ major. Note how the first finger replaces the nut in the F and F♯ chord diagrams as the E shape barre moves up the fretboard. As barre chords move higher up on the fretboard, the diagram will contain a number followed by *fr* which stands for *fret*. In Figure 3.14, the symbol 2fr indicates a barre across the second fret for the F♯ major chord.

It is possible to use other open chord shapes, such as E minor, A major, and A minor, to create more barred chords (Figure 3.15).

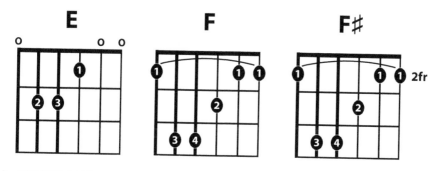

FIGURE 3.14
E Major Shape Barre

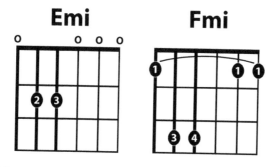

FIGURE 3.15
E Minor Shape Barre

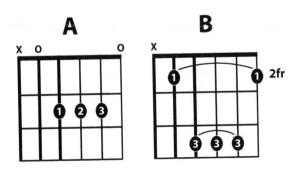

FIGURE 3.16
A Major Shape Barre

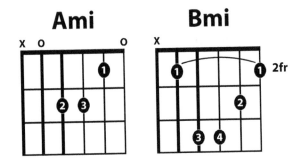

FIGURE 3.17
A Minor Shape Barre

When the A major shape is barred on the 2nd fret, it becomes a B major (Figure 3.16). The low E string is not used for the A major or A minor shape barre chord, resulting in a 5-string barre chord (Figure 3.17).

Barre Chord Tips

- Barre chords close to the nut are harder to play. Instead of starting on the 1st fret to play a F major barre chord, have students begin higher on the fretboard, such as the C major barre chord on the 8th fret.
- Make sure students place their finger close to the fret and not in the middle of the fret box.
- Students should use the side of the index finger to barre across the strings. This part of the finger is firmer than the flat part of the finger.
- The thumb should be placed parallel to the strings in the middle of the neck. This will give the player more leverage to hold down the strings.

Most teachers who incorporate guitar into their music classroom do so as part of whole-class instruction. As students gain experience with the guitar, some teachers will likely want to include other instruments such as bass, drum kit, and keyboard. Other teachers will prefer to stick with a whole-class guitar ensemble model for several reasons including limited access to other instruments, the structure of the class, and student preference. Whether you are teaching a whole-class guitar ensemble, or a mixed-instrumentation class, there is an opportunity for small group instruction. Students can form small groups to write original music or cover existing songs of their choice. Having students bring in material that they want to learn increases buy-in and can encourage students to engage with music at home.

ELECTRIC GUITAR

Most guitar ensembles and general music classrooms use acoustic guitars because they do not require amplification and are often the most cost-effective choice for school music programs. As students gain experience with the guitar, you may wish to include electric guitars in your classroom. This is especially true if you are incorporating other instruments such as keyboard, electric bass, and drum kit. One of the benefits of using an electric guitar is that they are often easier to play than an acoustic guitar. Because the action of the guitar (the distance between the strings and the fretboard) is lower on an electric guitar, students do not have to work as hard to push down the strings to play a chord. This is especially true for barre chords which can be difficult for beginning students to master.

Electric guitars require the use of a guitar amplifier (amp). When choosing a guitar amp, there are a few considerations including the loudness, built-in effects, speaker size, sound quality, circuit design, quality of construction, and cost. Guitar amps come in a variety of different wattages (a watt is a unit of power). Generally speaking, the higher the wattage, the more expensive the guitar amp is. Amp designs can range from 1 watt to over 100 watts. For most classrooms, an amp that is between 25 and 50 watts will produce plenty of sound without causing unwanted distortion at higher volume settings. For more information on amplifiers, check out Chapter 11: Live Sound and Recording.

One of the benefits of using electric guitars is that they are versatile instruments. Because electric guitars use an amp, and sometimes **effects pedals**, there is a wide variety of sounds that an electric guitar can make. There are times when you will want a more distorted sound when covering songs with your class or doing a songwriting activity. Imagine playing Nirvana's "Smells Like Teen Spirit" with a classroom of acoustic guitars; you can do it, but it will not sound as cool as playing that song with an electric guitar and some distortion. You can further manipulate the electric guitar's sound by using effects pedals. Effects pedals can impact the sound in many ways, including:

- manipulating the sound of the guitar to alter the output such as distortion or overdrive;
- altering the ambience of the sound with reverb and delay;
- changing the dynamics with volume or compression pedals;
- adding modulation effects such as chorus, phasers, and flangers; and
- filtering the sound with wah-wah pedals.

Guitar pedals allow the player to sculpt the sound in many ways. There are thousands of videos on YouTube that explain what each pedal does, and how pedals can be combined to achieve a desired effect.

DIFFERENTIATION

The guitar allows for a great deal of differentiation in popular music classes. The instrument comes in different sizes, weights, and even numbers of strings, accommodating a range of students with varying abilities. Students of widely different experience levels can also play the same songs using simplified, intermmediate, and advanced versions of chords on the guitar. Students can also perform strumming patterns of varying complexities at the same time. Here are some suggestions for engaging guitar students at three different levels.

Beginning Group

- Students play simplified three-string chords on the first beat of the chord changes.
- Students are divided into groups in which they are only responsible for playing one chord in the progression. While they are waiting to play their chord, they can still sing and follow along with the chord progression.
- Students perform with a partner and play every other chord. This allows ample time to make the changes between chords.
- Students play the root of the chord, functioning as bass players for the group.

Intermediate Group

- As students progress to learn the full chords, encourage them to play simplified strumming patterns at first, which will allow them to feel comfortable changing between chords.
- Encourage students to self-differentiate so they can make decisions about which chords to play, which strumming patterns are within their skill levels, and when they might want to substitute a power chord for a full barre chord.

Advanced Group

- Challenge advanced students who know how to play the full chords to substitute barre chords for open chords.

- Encourage students to use tablature to learn the melodic riffs, or use the appropriate pentatonic scale to start to improvise over the changes.
- Introduce your students to more advanced techniques such as **string bending, hammer-ons, pull-offs, slides,** etc. If you do not know what these techniques are, that is ok! There are thousands of YouTube videos that can teach students these techniques. Remember, you don't need to be the best guitar player in your classroom in order to teach the guitar!

CONCLUSION

The guitar is an instrument that allows students to play familiar songs quickly, without a great deal of formal training. By starting with simplified chords and strumming patterns, students can quickly begin to play the songs they know and love. Once students feel comfortable with three-string chords and simplified strumming patterns, they can progress to open chords, power chords, barre chords, and tablature. And remember, students of various abilities can play different parts of the same song, together in the same classroom. Whether a student is playing a three-string chord, an open chord, a power chord, or a barre chord, they can meaningfully participate in the music-making process.

Takeaways

- Students should play the guitar before they label the parts of the instrument.
- Using simplified chords and strumming patterns will allow students to get started quickly with success.
- Theory should be introduced *after* the students have started playing guitar.
- Students should self-differentiate their parts. Giving them options for strumming patterns and differentiated versions of chords instills a sense of autonomy and helps ensure they do not feel overwhelmed.
- Even if you are a beginning guitar player, you have a lot to offer your students through well-planned lessons, scaffolding, and differentiated instruction.

Discussion Questions

1. How are the approaches to teaching guitar outlined in this chapter similar to your experiences learning another instrument? How are they different?
2. What are some of the benefits of being able to accommodate learners of varying abilities in the same classroom?
3. What are some potential challenges to incorporating guitar instruction into your classroom or future classroom?

Note

1 NAMM, "Global Report."

Electric Bass

If you have not yet reviewed Chapter 2: Introduction to Guitar, Bass, and Ukulele, please do so before continuing with this chapter.

An electric bass player works together with a drummer to establish the groove, an important characteristic of most popular music genres. The instrument helps define the chord progression of a song and delivers low frequencies, contributing to a rich sonic texture. Virtually every style of music uses a bass player, and the function of the instrument is similar across genres. A student who learns the bass will have opportunities to play the instrument in a variety of settings.

BASICS

Parts of the Electric Bass

Many aspects of the electric bass are similar to the guitar: the strings span the length of the fretboard between the bridge and the nut; tuning keys or pegs at the headstock of the instrument adjust the tension of the strings; and dots located at the 3rd, 5th, 7th, 9th, 12th, and 15th frets serve as a visual guide for placing fingers on the fretboard (Figure 4.1). When a string on the electric bass is plucked, the pickups on the instrument sense vibrations from the string and generate an electric signal. The pickups consist of a coil wrapped around a magnetic pole. Almost all basses have pickup covers so that the coils are not exposed.

Tuning the Electric Bass

The pitches on the electric bass are the same as the four lowest sounding strings of the guitar, sounding one octave lower. They are also the same as the upright double bass that you would find in an orchestra. We recommend using a tuning app, such as GuitarTuna, or a clip-on instrument tuner to expedite the tuning process. If a tuner is not available, the bass can be tuned to match a piano

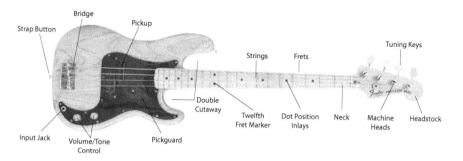

FIGURE 4.1
Parts of the Electric Bass

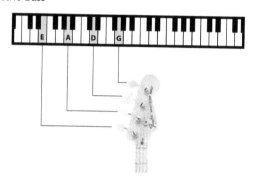

FIGURE 4.2
Tuning the Bass with a Piano

(Figure 4.2) or guitar. Students can memorize the order of the electric bass strings by shortening the guitar string acronyms presented in Chapter 3. The phrase Eddie Ate Dynamite, Good Bye Eddie becomes Eddie Ate Dynamite ... Good. Elephants And Dogs Grow Big Ears becomes Elephants And Dogs Grow. It is helpful to have one acronym that works for guitar and bass, especially if you are teaching both instruments in the same classroom.

Guitar as Bass
If you want to teach your students bass parts but do not have enough electric basses for everyone to have their own, you can use guitars to function as basses. Since the strings of the bass are the same as the lowest four strings on the guitar, students can use guitars to play bass parts as a class (Figure 4.3).

Choosing the Right Bass
While there are electric basses with more than four strings, we recommend that you use a four-string bass in the classroom because they are more accessible and easier to learn. Four-string basses are also more common and easier to find in smaller sizes such as 3/4 size and shorter scale basses. Since the

Guitar   Bass

FIGURE 4.3
Using the Guitar as a Bass

electric bass is larger than the guitar, a full-size electric bass will likely be too large for most elementary school students and even some middle and high school students. A full-size bass has approximately 20 frets and the fretboard is around 34 inches long. Smaller scale basses, such as the Fender Mustang or Bronco bass, have 19 frets and a fretboard that is 30 inches in length. You can also find "fretless" basses, but we do not recommend using those in the classroom as students will often become frustrated with intonation issues.

Holding the Bass
If students are playing a right-handed bass, they should rest the body of the instrument on their lap and hold the neck with the left hand. If students are standing, they should adjust the length of the strap so that the bass is in a comfortable playing position (Figure 4.4).

Playing Styles
Most bassists use a pick or their index and middle fingers to play individual notes on the bass, depending on the genre of music and the preference of the player. Many students will feel more comfortable using a pick initially, especially if they have previous experience playing the guitar. Playing the bass with your fingers results in a softer, warmer sound, while playing with a pick produces a harder, more percussive sound. Encourage students to explore both playing styles and let them "pick" the style they prefer. When using fingers to play the bass, students should rest their thumb on one of the bass pickups and use the index and middle fingers to lightly pluck the strings in alternating fashion (Figure 4.5).

We recommend starting with plucking the G string first to practice. When plucking the G string, the D string serves as a good kinesthetic reminder to stop the finger motion and reset. For some students, learning how to pluck the low E string first can throw them off because there is nothing to catch their finger after the E has been plucked. Make sure students are not plucking the strings too hard. Using a bass amplifier will allow students to hear the notes they are playing without much effort.

FIGURE 4.4
Sitting and Standing with the Bass

FIGURE 4.5
Plucking the Bass

Bass Knobs

All electric basses have knobs that adjust the volume and tone of the bass. These controls, in combination with the knobs on the bass amp, sculpt the overall tone of the sound. Most basses have either a master volume knob for all pickups, or two volume knobs that each control one pickup. The other knob (or two) will control the low and high frequencies that the bass produces. Since each bass is different, usually having between two to four knobs, it is best to look at the manual or search online to learn which knob controls each function of the bass. Generally, the knob(s) closest to the fretboard are the volume knobs and the knob(s) farthest from the fretboard adjust the tone.

> ### ALWAYS USE AN AMP!
>
> While it is possible to hear notes without using an amplifier, students should always use a bass amp when playing the electric bass. Practicing the bass without an amp will likely cause students to pluck the strings harder than they should in order to hear the notes, which can develop poor technique, especially if students are fingerpicking the strings. There is more information on bass amps at the end of this chapter.

Playing Bass Lines

One of the easiest ways to get started on the bass is to simply play the root note of the chords that the guitars and keyboards are playing. While more advanced bass parts will often include other chord tones and passing tones, starting with the root of the chords is a good place for beginners. There are a few ways to notate a bass line over a given chord progression, such as I–IV–V in Figure 4.6. This example uses slash notation with the individual notes

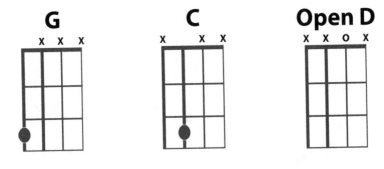

FIGURE 4.6
Playing Root Notes

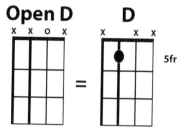

FIGURE 4.7

Two Ways of Playing the Same Note

indicated on the fretboard diagram. Each fret equals one half step, so the 3rd fret of the low E string is a G, as G is three half steps higher than E.

Different Ways to Play the Same Note

The note D may be produced by playing an open D string, as indicated on the left side of Figure 4.7. The same pitch can be achieved by playing the A string on the 5th fret (right side of Figure 4.7). The choice to play a note using a fretted or open string depends on comfort, context, – which note precedes or follows the pitch – and the type of rhythm that needs to be performed. Playing a note on the fretboard is easier to control rhythmically than playing a note on an open string because open strings will ring out and need to be muted with part of the left or right hand to stop the vibration. Visit http://popmusicped. com for a video on right- and left-hand techniques for shorter notes on open strings.

Bass Rhythms

Once students learn where to place notes on the fretboard, they can progress to learning more advanced rhythms on the bass. Just as the guitar uses strum patterns to provide rhythmic complexity to a chord progression, the bass can use rhythmic playing to add a new element to the song. Sometimes the bass and the guitar play the same rhythmic parts, and sometimes the bass plays a different rhythmic part to provide contrast to rhythmic patterns provided by the keyboard and guitar. The process of creating these rhythmic accompaniments is known as comping. Figure 4.8 illustrates various comping patterns that students can play on the bass as well as an example of rhythmic iconic notation.

APPROACHES

Bass Lines

The bass player is responsible for providing a bass line in most popular music settings. The bass line helps establish the key of a song by emphasizing the root of chord progressions, often through the repetition of a rhythmic pattern,

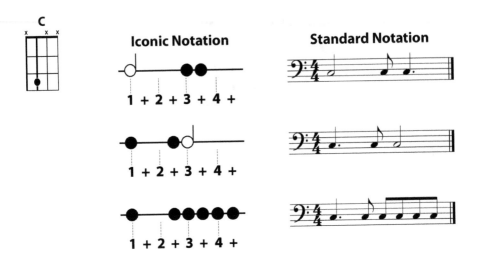

FIGURE 4.8
Rhythmic Accompaniments (Comping Patterns)

such as the ones identified in the previous section. The combination of the bass line and drum set part creates the groove that is an important characteristic of popular music genres. A good rule of thumb for beginning bassists is to match the bass rhythms with the bass drum part. The electric bass can function in many ways, including playing the changes, the beat, a walking bass, or a **riff**.

Playing the Changes
In most popular music songs, the bass player's job is to play the root note of each chord in the harmonic progression (changes). As detailed above, these changes often happen each measure, but can happen every other measure, or multiple times per measure. In 4/4 meter, a bass player will often play the root of the chord on beat one, and will then repeat the root or play the 5th or the octave on the remaining beats. The bass part is relatively simple when just playing the changes, but simplicity is part of the power of the bass.

Playing the Beat
Playing the beat simply means that a note is sounded on each beat, or twice per beat (Figure 4.9). This usually entails the bass player playing the root note on the beat, or alternating between the root and 5th, or the root and octave.

Walking Bass
A walking bass line is a pattern that outlines the chord quality and includes passing tones (stepwise motion between two different chord tones) and neighbor tones (stepwise motion away from and returning to the starting chord tone). The part usually starts with the root of the chord on beat one and a chord tone on beat three. Beats two and four can contain passing,

Quarter Note Pattern   Eighth Note Pattern

FIGURE 4.9
Playing the Beat

FIGURE 4.10
Walking Bass Line

neighboring, or other chord tones that fill out the line. The last note of the measure often leads to the next measure by a half step. While many beginners will want to use a "one fret per finger" approach, more experienced bassists often use fingers 1, 2, and 4 (instead of 1, 2, and 3) for certain walking bass or melodic lines. Figure 4.10 illustrates a walking bass line over a dominant 7th chord that is typical of the blues.

Playing a Riff

The bass can also be used to play a short melodic phrase or **riff**. Examples of famous bass riffs include "Money" by Pink Floyd and "Another One Bites the Dust" by Queen. Melodic bass parts are often notated using bass tablature.

Bass Intervals

The interval between each string on the bass is a fourth (e.g., E to A, A to D, and D to G). This means that the relationship between intervals is the same across the entire fretboard. Since many popular music songs use I, IV, and V chords, understanding how fourths and fifths map onto a fretboard is an important concept for a bass player.

Playing Fourths

To play a note that is a fourth higher on the bass, students simply play the next higher string on the same fret. Notes played on adjacent strings on the same fret will be a fourth apart. So, if students are playing a G on the third fret of the E string and want to play a C (a fourth higher), they simply play the third fret of the A string (Figure 4.11).

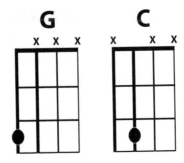

FIGURE 4.11
Relationship of a Fourth: One String Higher, Same Fret

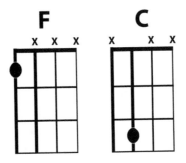

FIGURE 4.12
Relationship of a Fifth: One String Higher, Two Frets Higher

Playing Fifths
The relationship between a root note and the fifth is one string higher and two frets higher. In Figure 4.12, F is the root and C is the fifth. The C is one string, and two frets higher than the F.

Playing Octaves
The relationship between octaves on a bass is two strings higher and two frets higher. In Figure 4.13, F is the root and F an octave higher is two strings and two frets away. We recommend using fingers 1 and 4 (the pinky) for these octaves as it might be too much of a stretch for students to use fingers 1 and 3.

Bass Patterns
Figure 4.14 shows two common patterns that students can practice to develop their bass technique. One of the best ways for students to improve their bass skills is to learn riffs and patterns from their favorite songs.

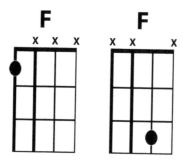

FIGURE 4.13
Relationship of an Octave: Two Strings Higher, Two Frets Higher

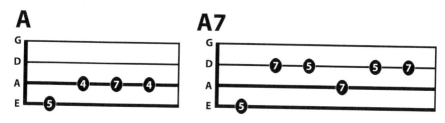

FIGURE 4.14
Common Bass Patterns

BASS AMPLIFIERS

As previously mentioned, it is important to use a bass amplifier when playing the bass to avoid poor technique. For even more information on bass amplifiers, visit http://popmusicped.com.

Bass Amp Head
This part of the bass amp contains most of the electronics, including the inputs for plugging in the bass, a preamp (to manipulate and shape the sound), and a power amp (to boost the signal). A bass amp head, also called simply a head, does not produce any audible sound unless it is connected to a speaker cabinet.

Bass Speaker Cabinet
This is a box that contains the speakers. The cabinet does not plug into the wall, but instead receives a signal from the powered speaker head and works together with the bass amp head in a stack.

Combo Amp
Combo amps combine the head and the cabinet into one unit and are ideal for most classrooms. With combo amps, you don't have to worry about

connecting the head to the cabinet. With a combo amp, you just plug it in and you are ready to go!

Amplifier Head Knobs

In addition to the input where the bass is plugged into the amp head, heads will always have a series of knobs that can be adjusted to sculpt the sound. Depending on the style of music, students will want to adjust the knobs to find a timbre that works for them. Most amp heads have a bass, mid, and treble knobs. The bass knob regulates the low-end frequencies and helps to provide a deep presence to the sound. The mid knob helps regulate the middle frequencies which fill out the sound. The treble knob regulates the higher frequencies and provides a brightness to the sound. While many beginning bass players use a "set it and forget it" technique with most of the knobs at middle range adjusting the knobs on the amp can help sculpt the sound and give students the best tone for the style of music they want to play.

Gain Versus Volume

You and your students might notice that as you explore knobs on the amp, you can make the sound louder by turning up both the gain (sometimes labeled *drive*) and the volume knob. So, what's the difference? Basically, the gain is a reference for the signal strength that is coming through the amp or microphone, and volume is a measurement of sound. So as the signal comes from the guitar or bass into the amplifier, it isn't very loud. The amplifier boosts the signal – this is the gain. The volume knob then adjusts the decibels (i.e., loudness) of that sound. Increasing the gain might cause distortion (which is often a desired effect). If students want to add distortion to their sound, but don't want the amp to get louder, they should turn the gain (or drive) up and turn the volume down.

DIFFERENTIATION

There are opportunities to differentiate a bass part for students who are not able to use two hands to play the instrument. Since the open strings on the bass correspond to beginning chords on the guitar (E, A, D, and G), students who might not be able to use their left hand to hold down a string on a fret can play the open strings whenever the song calls for an E, Emi, A, Ami, D, Dmi, G, or Gmi chord. Playing an open string also gives students a break from holding down the strings if their fingers hurt. If a student is not able to use their right hand to pluck the bass strings, it is still possible to play the bass by using **finger tapping**. Finger tapping is a technique where you strike down on the string with your fingers to create a sound. It is possible to play bass lines and even melodies one-handed using finger tapping. Students with limited physical ability may also perform the role of the bass player using virtual instruments on touch screen devices or with a keyboard bass synthesizer. Because the bass player typically plays one note at a time, these devices allow a student to perform this role using just one finger.

CONCLUSION

It is relatively easy for students to begin learning the bass. Since the bass part for beginners often just requires that you play the root note of the chord, this can lead teachers to believe the bass is an instrument for those students who are not very good on the guitar. However, just because the bass might be an easier instrument to learn at first, it does not mean that it should be a consolation for those students who have a difficult time learning guitar. The bass player is often in a support role, so it is important that the students on the bass are sensitive musicians with good listening abilities. In your classroom, you will find that some students are drawn to the bass and become more excited about learning the bass than the guitar. We recommend playing bass lines and bass parts on the acoustic guitar with all of your students, especially initially, so that your students can get a sense of how the bass functions within a popular music ensemble.

Takeaways

- Students can experience instant success with the bass.
- Always use an amplifier when playing the bass to avoid plucking too hard.
- Bass players can start by playing the roots of the chord changes, and then advance to riffs or walking bass lines as they become more familiar with the instrument.
- All students can practice the bass part on their guitars using the four lowest sounding strings (E, A, D, and G).
- Students who require accommodations may pluck the open strings or use finger tapping techniques.

Discussion Questions

1. What is the role of the bass in popular music?
2. What are some opportunities for accommodations and adaptations when playing the bass?
3. What are some considerations to keep in mind when first learning to play the bass?
4. Why might some students prefer to play the bass over the guitar?

Ukulele

If you have not yet reviewed Chapter 2: Introduction to Guitar, Bass, and Ukulele, please do so before continuing with this chapter.

This iconic Hawaiian instrument originated in Portugal and was brought to the islands by Portuguese immigrants in the late 1800s. A popular instrument due to its compact size, the ukulele has become a standard classroom instrument in K-12 music programs across the United States. The ukulele (abbreviated as "uke") is a small instrument that is lightweight and fits well into the hands of students of all ages. It only uses four strings and is smaller than a guitar, making it easier for beginners to play. It is also more affordable than many other instruments and a popular choice for general music classrooms and school popular music programs. Some chord shapes transfer from the ukulele directly to the guitar, so students may find it easier to play the guitar once they have learned the ukulele.

BASICS

There are many similarities between the ukulele and other fretted instruments. Like the guitar, the ukulele is a chordal instrument that can also play melodic lines. The ukulele has many of the same parts as the guitar as well (Figure 5.1).

The smallest and most common ukulele is the soprano; most students will be able play chords on this instrument comfortably. The next largest is the concert ukulele, followed by the tenor, baritone, and bass ukuleles. The different sizes of the instruments are helpful in accommodating children with a variety of hand sizes; the wider frets of the tenor ukulele are more easily accessible for larger children than the smaller soprano ukulele (Figure 5.2).

The soprano, concert, and tenor ukuleles all use the same tuning, so all three sizes can be used in the classroom without changing chord diagrams or other forms of iconic notation. The tunings for the baritone and bass ukulele are discussed later in this chapter. Unlike the strings of the guitar and bass,

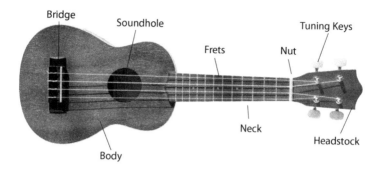

FIGURE 5.1
Parts of the Ukulele

FIGURE 5.2
Different Sizes of Ukuleles
Photo courtesy of Kris Gilbert

which sound from lowest to highest pitch as the strings are ordered from left to right, the ukulele's G string is higher in pitch than the C and E strings to the right of it (Figure 5.3).

For students who already play guitar, you can explain that the ukulele is strung five frets higher than the top four strings of the guitar (Figure 5.4). This

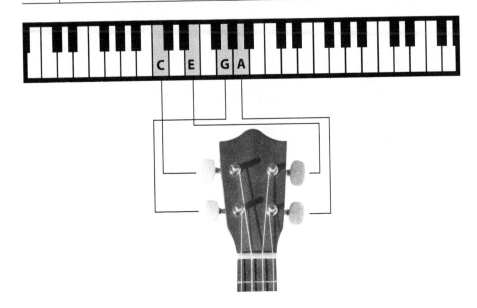

FIGURE 5.3
Tuning for Soprano, Concert, and Tenor Ukuleles

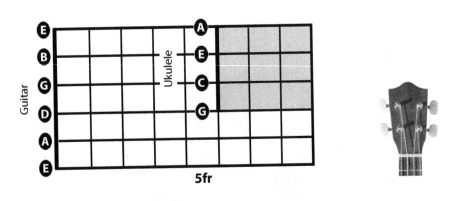

FIGURE 5.4
Similarities between Ukulele and Guitar

means that you can use many of the same ukulele chord shapes on the guitar, just five frets higher. Figure 5.9 illustrates some of these chord similarities.

A baritone ukulele, while less common in music classrooms, is often used in ukulele ensembles. The tuning for the baritone ukulele is D–G–B–E, which matches the tuning for the highest pitched four strings of the guitar exactly. For this reason, students who already play guitar often find it easier to learn the baritone ukulele since they are familiar with many of the chord shapes. In Figure 5.5, you can see that the D chord shape on the baritone ukulele is the

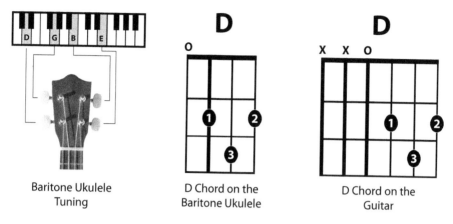

| Baritone Ukulele Tuning | D Chord on the Baritone Ukulele | D Chord on the Guitar |

FIGURE 5.5
Common Strings and Chords for Baritone Ukulele and Guitar

same as the D chord shape on the guitar. The baritone ukulele also provides a lower timbre for adding different tone colors to the ensemble.

The bass ukulele fits well in any popular music ensemble. Unlike the full-size electric bass which might be too large for some students to play comfortably, the bass ukulele is easy to hold and is tuned like a full-size bass (E–A–D–G). As a reminder, this is the same tuning as the four lowest strings of the guitar. The strings on the bass ukulele are thicker than those on a full-sized electric bass to compensate for the shorter scale of the fretboard.

Holding the Ukulele
Ukulele players do not typically wear a strap, so the instrument should be held against the chest with the forearm of the strumming hand gently pressed against the body of the instrument (Figure 5.6). However, music teachers who are holding their ukuleles for hours each day may want to use a ukulele strap when they teach. Since every person is a different shape and size, each player will need to find a comfortable holding position that works for them. Like the guitar, the thumb of the fretting hand should be behind the neck of the ukulele, with the tips of the fingers ready to press the fretboard. Like the hand position for playing the keyboard, the fingers should be arched to avoid hitting other strings when pressing down on the fretboard.

Ukulele players do not typically use a pick, and there are various ways to strum the ukulele strings with the strumming hand. One common strumming approach is to use the thumb to strum down and the index finger to strum up. Another popular approach is to use the nail of the index finger on downstrokes and the nail of the thumb on upstrokes. You can have students try different ways of strumming and use the style that is most comfortable to them. If students prefer to use a pick to strum the strings, they should use a felt or leather pick as hard plastic picks can damage the strings and remove some of the

FIGURE 5.6
Holding a Ukulele

FIGURE 5.7
Strumming a Ukulele

warmth of the ukulele sound. It is best to strum where the fretboard meets the body of the instrument, or above the fretboard itself. Students should avoid playing too close to the bridge at the bottom of the ukulele (Figure 5.7).

Ukulele Chords

The C chord is a logical first choice to introduce to students. Like the simplified three-string G chord on the guitar, the C chord on the ukulele can be played with one finger on the third fret of the highest string. Similarly, the A minor

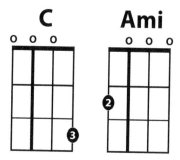

FIGURE 5.8
First Ukulele Chords

chord can be played with one finger on the second fret of the G string. There are many songs that students can play by using just one chord (e.g., Aretha Franklin's "Chain of Fools," War's "Low Rider," and Bob Marley's "Get Up, Stand Up"). Once students have learned one or two chords, have them dive in and play songs right away. One tip for switching between these two chords is to hover the fingers over the string and fret of the next chord so that the hand is in position to play the next chord. Using the third finger to play the C chord allows the player to easily transition to the second finger to play the A minor chord (Figure 5.8).

There are other ukulele chords that utilize an identical or very similar hand structure to guitar chords. For example, the D chord on the ukulele uses the same fingerings as the A chord on the guitar, and the G chord on the ukulele uses the same fingerings as the D chord on the guitar (Figure 5.9).

Power Chords
The guitar chapter of this book discusses power chords in depth. As a reminder, a power chord utilizes the root and the 5th of the chord. Since the 3rd is omitted, power chords do not have a chord quality (major or minor). Students can play power chords on the ukulele as well. Since the two strings closest to the nose are G and C (with G being the higher-pitched note), their interval is a perfect fifth. This means that if students play the two strings closest to their nose together, they are playing a C power chord! Figure 5.10 shows some other power chords on the ukulele. These chords can be substituted for full versions of either major or minor chords.

Another way to play power chords on the ukulele is to play the two strings closest to the toes (E and A) in the same power chord shape used for the two-string E and A guitar power chord (Figure 5.11).

Tablature for Ukulele
As discussed in Chapter 2, tablature is a form of notation that uses numbers and lines to indicate which frets and strings should be played. Since ukuleles have four strings, its tablature looks like the diagram in Figure 5.12.

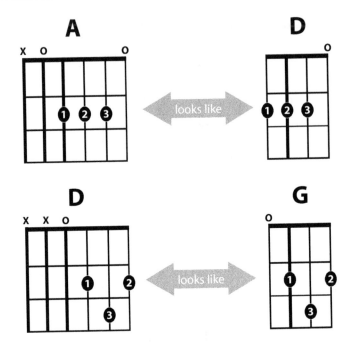

FIGURE 5.9
Common Chord Shapes for Guitar (left) and Ukulele (right)

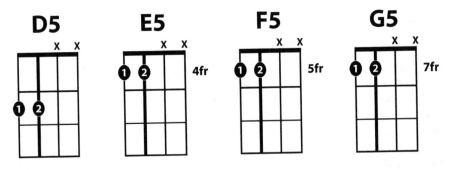

FIGURE 5.10
Power Chords for Ukulele

By expressing melodic lines in tablature notation, you may provide instant access for students to solo and play lead lines. You can also have some members of the class play the chords of a song while other students play the melodic lines.

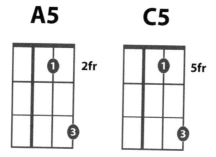

FIGURE 5.11
Power Chords on the E and A Strings

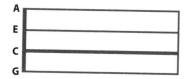

FIGURE 5.12
Ukulele Tablature

Soloing for Ukulele

The ukulele player may be featured as a soloist, improvising first with simple two-note solos, and then moving to four-note solos and the pentatonic scale. Figure 5.13 provides diagrams to help beginning improvisers identify the placement of their fingers to perform two-note and four-note solos in A minor on the ukulele. A soloist may start by using a two-note solo using the open A string and the note on the third fret of the A string which is a C. Once the soloist feels comfortable using those two notes to solo, they can add two more notes by playing the open E and A strings, and the notes on the third frets of the E and A strings to take a four-note solo. A good **backing track** to use for these solos is any song or play-along in the key of A minor.

Students can learn a pentatonic scale pattern and then move the shape around the fretboard to play in different keys. There are five different patterns for playing minor and major pentatonic scales on the ukulele. Students can start by learning one shape and then expand to incorporate different scale patterns as their skill level grows.

Barre Chords

Barre chords involve holding down multiple strings at the same time with one finger. In many barre chords, the first finger replaces the function of the nut and acts as a movable capo. In Figure 5.15, the first finger barres across all the strings on the 1st fret to turn the C chord into a C♯ chord.

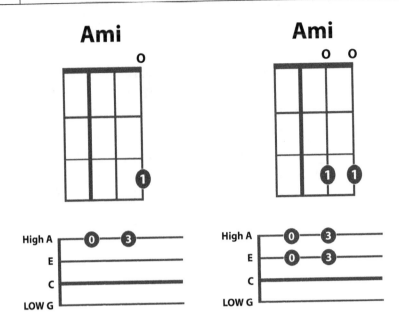

FIGURE 5.13

Two-Note and Four-Note Solo Diagrams in A minor

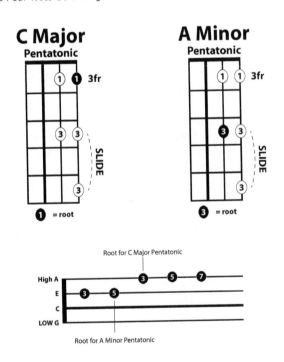

FIGURE 5.14

One Scale Pattern for Major and Minor Pentatonic Scales

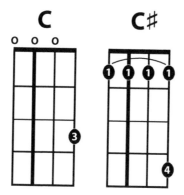

FIGURE 5.15

C Chord and C♯ Barre Chord Diagrams

APPROACHES

Uke Jam Sessions

Uke jam sessions are a fun way to engage students and community members in creative music-making experiences. These gatherings, whether in a school or community setting, usually include play-alongs that provide the chords, lyrics, and backing track to a popular song. Check out the YouTube channels of Jill Reese, Spencer Hale, Uke Play-Alongs, and The Ukulaliens for a variety of free ukulele play-alongs. There are also apps, such as Ukeoke, that offer customizable play-along videos where users can change the keys and tempos of play-alongs. These apps often require a monthly subscription or a one-time fee. Visit http://popmusicped.com for links to these ukulele resources.

Differentiation in Ensemble Playing

There are several opportunities for differentiation and accommodation using the ukulele. Beginning students can simply play the chords they know on beat one while using the rest of the measure to prepare for the next chord. Beginning students can also play two-string power chords in place of more difficult chords. Intermediate students can play the chord progressions while experimenting with different strumming patterns, and advanced students can play melodic lines while reading tab and incorporate barre chords as appropriate.

The ukulele can also be a welcome addition to a popular music ensemble with other rock band instruments. Many popular artists are incorporating the ukulele into their songs, including Jason Mraz, Twenty One Pilots, and Taylor Swift. Students can also take a song that does not have a ukulele part and arrange it for a ukulele ensemble. Since the ukulele is a relatively quiet instrument, having multiple ukuleles in an ensemble and/or amplifying the sound of an acoustic/electric ukulele can prevent the instrument from becoming drowned out by the guitars, electric bass, and drum kit. Acoustic/electric ukuleles are usually priced $150–$250 and are useful to have as a teacher, to amplify your own playing or in performance settings where increased volume is desired.

CONCLUSION

The ukulele is a compact instrument that fits well in the hands of younger students and is easily accessible for all learners. The instrument only has four strings, and it is lightweight and affordable, making it a great addition to general music classrooms and popular music ensembles. The uke may be used as a substitute for guitar and bass, or performed in addition to these other fretted instruments. The uke shares many similarities with the guitar in its design, playing technique, notation, and learning approaches. Like a guitarist, the ukulele player uses iconic notation such as chord diagrams and tablature, and the instrument may be used to teach improvisation, songwriting, and ensemble playing. The versatility and accessibility of the ukulele make it an increasingly popular choice among K-12 music teachers.

Takeaways

- The ukulele is becoming more popular to use in the classroom due to its size, ease of learning, and affordability.
- Starting with one-finger chords provides students with instant access to the songs they love.
- There are several different sizes of ukuleles, and the soprano, concert, and tenor are tuned the same way.
- As students become more experienced, they can incorporate power chords and barre chords along with playing melodic lines using tablature.

Discussion Questions

1. What are the benefits of including ukulele in music classrooms?
2. What are the ways that you might be able to differentiate instruction while teaching the ukulele?
3. How might ukulele instruction be different in the elementary grades as compared to middle and high school?

Keyboard

Keyboard instruments have been a central component of music teaching
and learning for centuries, but the techniques and approaches to
learning this instrument in a popular music setting are likely unfamiliar
to many classically trained music educators. While most music teachers may
have learned to play piano through method books and technical exercises
expressed in five-line staff notation, there are other approaches to learning the
keyboard that may be more appropriate for students of popular music. You
may wish to reconceptualize this familiar instrument with a beginner's mind,
as you consider new methods for learning the keyboard in ways that align with
popular music practices.

BASICS

Keyboard Notation
A keyboard player in a popular music ensemble often relies on lead sheets and
chord charts instead of five-line staff notation. Lead sheets provide the chords,
rhythm, melody, and lyrics for a song; this information allows players of a
variety of instruments to contribute to the group using a single notated part.
In addition to lead sheets, there are several types of iconic notation which
provide visual representations of the keyboard, highlighting which notes to
play and specific fingerings to use. The first keyboard in Figure 6.1 displays
the notes of a C major triad (C, E, and G), highlighted for the player, using the
first, third, and fifth fingers of the right hand. The second keyboard represents
the notes in an A minor pentatonic scale (A, C, D, E, G) with the suggested
fingering pattern for this scale. These keyboard diagrams can also be placed
above slash notation, as seen in Figure 6.2. By highlighting the notes that are
played, students who do not read five-line staff notation can still understand
which notes to play for a chord or scale. Visit http://popmusicped.com for
links to song charts that use this form of iconic notation for keyboard.

A keyboard part may also be expressed through piano roll notation. In
this form of iconic notation, a representation of the keyboard is rotated on its
side and shaded notes correspond with keys (pitches). This piano roll representation is common in recording software and many **digital audio workstations**

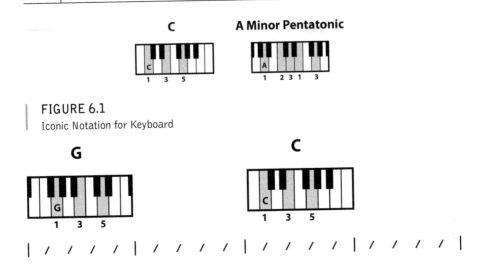

FIGURE 6.1
Iconic Notation for Keyboard

FIGURE 6.2
Iconic Notation for a Chord Progression

(DAWs) (see Chapter 10). While it is uncommon for keyboard players to read a part using piano roll notation, it is useful to understand how this notation works in sound recording projects, as MIDI information may be easily edited (pitch, duration, velocity, etc.) using this system (Figure 6.3).

Another type of iconic notation that is becoming increasingly popular for the keyboard is the "falling notes" visualization. Made popular through the video game Guitar Hero and more recently through the software Synthesia, this type of iconic notation displays the notes descending onto a keyboard with the duration of the note represented by the length of the shapes. Note in Figure 6.4 the similarities between this video game-style of notation and the piano roll notation, which is nearly identical and simply rotated on its side.

The software application Yousician combines elements of iconic and staff notation by color-coding notes, placing them on the music staff, and using various sized rectangles to match the duration of the note (Figure 6.5). The software also provides a color-coded visualization of the keyboard to help the player identify pitches and know which fingers to use (e.g., green pitches are always played with thumbs). Yousician allows the user the option to view traditional five-line staff notation, which may be helpful for teachers who wish to introduce this form of notation to students through familiar repertoire.

Technique

Electric keyboard technique is similar to playing the acoustic piano. If you have taken piano lessons, the tips that you likely remember of curving the fingers, relaxing the arms, and playing with the pads of fingers are the same for the keyboard. Recommendations for piano-playing posture may be slightly different for the keyboard as many keyboardists in popular music ensembles stand (and move!)

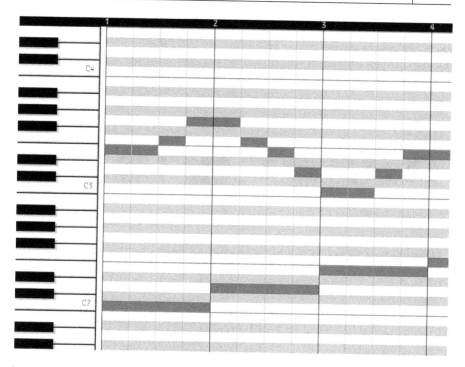

FIGURE 6.3
Piano Roll Notation

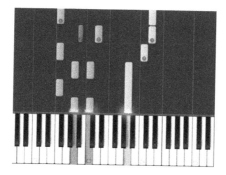

FIGURE 6.4
Synthesia Notation
Photo retrieved from *https://synthesia.app* and reprinted with permission

as they play. One technical note is the difference in how fingers are numbered on the keyboard compared to the guitar. Unlike guitar technique, in which the index finger is described as your first finger, a keyboardist's first finger is the thumb. This can be challenging for students with previous experience playing guitar, but visuals such as Figure 6.6 can help minimize confusion.

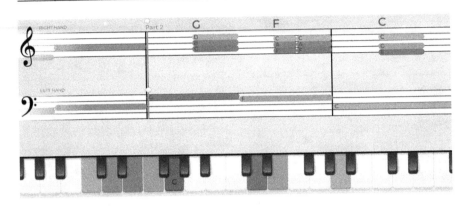

FIGURE 6.5
Yousician Notation
Photo retrieved from Yousician.com and reprinted with permission

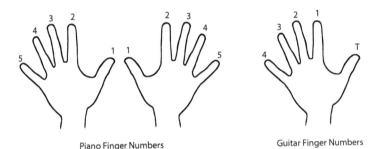

Piano Finger Numbers   Guitar Finger Numbers

FIGURE 6.6
Piano and Guitar Finger Numbers

Touch-Sensitive Keys versus Weighted Keys

Most modern classroom keyboards have **touch-sensitive** keys that register the velocity of the key strike (i.e., how hard the key is pressed). This allows the keyboardist to play softer by touching the keys more lightly and to play louder by striking the keys with more force. There are some keyboards without touch sensitivity which register one level of pressure across the entire keyboard regardless of how lightly or firmly the key is played. Touch-sensitive keyboards are better for the classroom because they help students to demonstrate dynamic contrast. There are also keyboards with **weighted keys** which more accurately replicate the feel of an acoustic piano. Keyboards with weighted keys are often more expensive than those without weighted keys but offer a more realistic feel, similar to playing an acoustic piano. For the classroom, nonweighted, touch-sensitive keyboards are a good balance between performance and affordability.

Keyboard Stands

While keyboard players typically sit down to practice, it is common for them to stand for a performance. The height of a keyboard should be adjusted to fit the standing performer. To determine the desired height of the keyboard stand, students should stand with arms relaxed at their side and elbows bent at a 90-degree angle. The keys of the keyboard should ideally be at the same level to allow for comfortable playing. This means that the keyboard stand should be 4–6 inches shorter than this level to accommodate for the thickness of the keyboard when placed upon the stand. Most keyboard stands have several height adjustments. You will find that some adjustment mechanisms are easier to use than others.

Sustain Pedals

Most keyboards will come with a **sustain pedal**. Some are single-piece plastic pedals, while others include a metal pedal that replicates the look and feel of an acoustic piano. While it is preferable to give more advanced players the option to use a pedal when they play, the reality is that in most school-based popular music ensembles, using a keyboard pedal is optional. Since the pedals are not attached to the keyboard and need to be plugged in separately, it is not uncommon for pedals to become lost or broken within the first year of buying the keyboard. Replacing sustain pedals is a matter of preference, budget, and skill level of the students.

Synthesizers

You have probably heard of **synthesizers,** or *synths,* and might use the term to refer to all electric keyboards, but they are not synonymous. A synth is the device that creates (synthesizes) sounds and may replicate acoustic and electronic instruments. The keyboard refers simply to the black and white keys of the device, not the synthesizer itself. There are also digitally sampled keyboards which use sounds that are sampled recordings of actual keyboards and pianos (Steinway, Fender Rhodes, etc.). These digitally sampled keyboards sound more lifelike, but are more expensive. Most of the time, when you think about a keyboard that you would use in the classroom, you are thinking of a combination keyboard and synthesizer. There are keyboards without synthesizers; MIDI controllers for example, can include keyboards but not always synthesizers. MIDI controllers typically produce sound through a computer or other interface. There are also synthesizers that do not have keyboards. These synthesizers allow you to sculpt the sound that you hear by adjusting the wave form, the envelope, and other parameters of the sound with dials, switches, and other controls.

Mini Keyboards

In recent years, mini keyboards such as the Casio SA76 have become very popular in classrooms because of the affordability of these devices and the minimal amount of storage space they require. Here are some things to consider when deciding whether to use mini keyboards in the classroom.

Positives

- *Price.* At around $49, mini keyboards are half the cost of an entry-level keyboard.
- *Storage.* Mini keyboards are much easier to store than full-size keyboards.
- *Setup.* Students can play mini keyboards on their laps without a stand.
- *Practicing at home.* Students can easily take mini keyboards home to practice.
- *Mobility.* Unlike a keyboard lab setup, teachers who "teach from a cart" and travel to different classrooms can easily transport these keyboards.

Challenges

- *Technique.* Since the keys are a smaller width, students may not use the appropriate fingering (e.g., students may play a root position triad chord with their thumb, first finger, and middle finger).
- *Transfer.* Playing on a full-size keyboard or piano after learning on a mini-keyboard will take some adjustment.

APPROACHES

The Role of the Keyboard Player

Most keyboard players in popular music ensembles play chords in the right hand and roots of the chords or a bass line in the left hand. The keyboard player does not need to play the melody of the song because the vocalist is singing this part. For beginner keyboard players, mastering basic root position triad shapes – played with the thumb, middle finger, and pinky – is the key to being able to play many songs right away. The I–V–vi–IV chord progression in Figure 6.7 demonstrates how each of these individual chords may be performed using the same shape. This means that if students can play one chord shape, they can play many chords, harmonic progressions, and full songs.

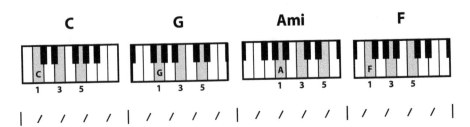

FIGURE 6.7
Performing Four Chords with One Shape

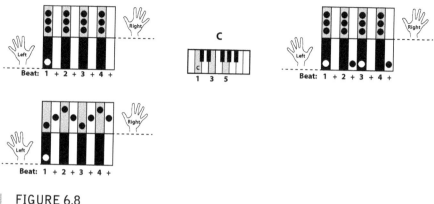

FIGURE 6.8

Comping Patterns

Image courtesy of Little Kids Rock

Comping Patterns

Just as guitarists play strumming patterns to add a rhythmic element to chords progressions, keyboard players can **comp** rhythms and patterns to match the feel of the song. For example, keyboard players can perform an arpeggiation (chord tones, one at a time), block chords (simultaneous chord tones), or combinations of the two. Little Kids Rock developed the visual patterns shown in Figure 6.8 to demonstrate the role of the right and left hand in paying different comping patterns. This rhythmic iconic notation is read from left to right and is subdivided by eighth notes. The beats are written under the diagram. The black notes represent the three notes of a triad (usually scale degrees 1, 3, and 5) in the right hand while the white dot represents the root of the chord played in the left hand. In the bottom example, the right hand is arpeggiating the chord while the left hand plays the root.

These iconic notation chord diagrams and rhythm patterns for the keyboard are designed to enable students to perform chords and rhythms on the keyboard quickly without the need of five-line staff notation. Because comping patterns in popular music are often repetitive, these rhythms may be applied to an entire chord progression of a song, allowing the student to perform their role as a keyboardist in a popular music ensemble. Students can also create their own comping patterns by listening to recordings and imitating what they hear.

KEYBOARD FEATURES

While the electric keyboard and the acoustic piano share many similarities, the keyboard has additional features that make it a great instrument for the classroom.

- **Tuning**. Unlike an acoustic piano, an electric keyboard never needs to be tuned.

- **Headphones**. Keyboard players can use headphones to practice their parts individually without interrupting other classmates. When it is time to play with the entire ensemble, the students can unplug their headphones and be a part of the band.
- **Transposition**. Almost all keyboards are capable of transposition. This allows your keyboard players to transpose difficult chord progressions into more comfortable keys.
- **Backing tracks**. Most keyboards come with a variety or backing tracks and drum beats which may be used as a practice tool, or as part of a songwriting activity.
- **Keyboard sounds**. Electric keyboards can recreate hundreds of sounds, called patches that are useful in popular music ensembles. If students are covering a song that has orchestral strings in it, the keyboard can replicate this part.
- **MIDI**. MIDI keyboards can connect to computers and iPads to provide a wide range of recording and production possibilities. For more on MIDI, check out Chapter 10: Digital Audio Workstations.

Jam Cards and Key Cards

The nonprofit organization Little Kids Rock developed a tool called Jam Cards;[1] this is a valuable resource for teaching keyboard players in a popular music ensemble. Jam Cards are visual guides that illustrate the notes of a chord, scale, or harmonic progression. The organization Musical Futures developed a similar tool called Key Cards.[2] Students simply slide the card behind the keys of a keyboard and colored bars indicate which notes to play. The cards provide instant transpositions for chords, scales, and progressions by moving the card to a different starting place on the keyboard. This is especially useful if a keyboard player is performing an improvised solo using a specific scale. Figure 6.9 shows examples of both methods.

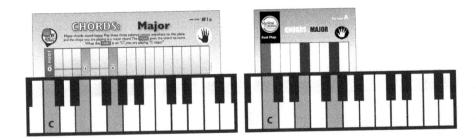

FIGURE 6.9
Little Kids Rock Jam Card (left) and Musical Futures Key Card (right)
Images courtesy of Little Kids Rock and Musical Futures International

Visit popmusicped.com for video examples and explanations of basic keyboard techniques.

Identifying Pitches on a Keyboard

One of the first concepts that a new keyboard player must learn is the pattern of the note names for the keyboard. There are certain tricks for remembering the note names of each key. The two black keys look like chopsticks and the note immediately to the left of the chopsticks is a C. The three black keys look like the tines of a fork and the note immediately to the left of the fork is an F (Figure 6.10).

Even with these tools, beginning players may struggle to remember the names of keys on the keyboard. Using stickers or dry erase markers to label the note names of the keys provides instant access to this information for students. One of the benefits of using dry erase markers on plastic keys is that the marker will eventually rub off. If students write the names of the pitches on the keyboard themselves, they will learn the note names quicker than they would have learned them if the teacher provided this information. Eventually, students will realize they no longer need to write note names on the keys, at which point they will have fully learned to identify pitches on a keyboard.

Moving from Iconic to Five-Line Staff Notation

The Jam Cards, comping pattern visuals, and the shaded in chord and scale patterns described above are all examples of iconic notation that can be used to teach the keyboard. However, if one of your desired outcomes is for students to be able to read traditional five-line staff notation then it is useful to combine both the iconic and staff notation side by side. Students will begin to make connections between the two forms of notation and understand how the music they are performing is expressed with five-line staff notation. Little Kids Rock has several examples of incorporating iconic and five-line staff notation together available on their Jam Zone website. Two examples are shown in Figure 6.11.

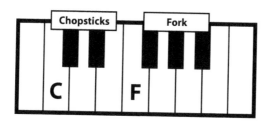

FIGURE 6.10
Chopsticks and Fork Visual Guide
Image courtesy of Little Kids Rock

FIGURE 6.11
A Comping Pattern and Triad Expressed in Iconic and Staff Notation
Image courtesy of Little Kids Rock

DIFFERENTIATION

There are many opportunities for differentiation when teaching the keyboard. As mentioned earlier, the use of stickers or dry erase markers to identify the notes on the keyboards allows less experienced students to immediately recognize patterns, reducing anxiety about not knowing where notes are placed on the keyboard. Once the keys are marked with stickers or dry erase markers, students can use a simple triad shape to play most basic chords. Moving this chord hand shape around the keyboard will give students confidence and the muscle memory necessary to feel comfortable on the instrument. As students gain familiarity with the basic chord shape, they can add harmonic extensions such as 7th chords as well as passing tones when switching between chords. As the types of chords that they can play become more advanced, so too can the comping patterns that they use to match the rhythms in the song. Most beginning students will either play the triad chords on the beat or simply as whole notes on beat one of the measure. Students with more experience can add complex rhythmic comping patterns that incorporate arpeggiation and other melodic ideas. These comping patterns can grow to include walking bass lines (for example, the introduction to Journey's "Don't Stop Believing"). More advanced students can also start to challenge themselves by playing songs in the original keys instead of using the transposition. Advanced students can experiment with playing melodic lines or improvising in the right hand while playing the chords in the left hand.

In addition to these suggestions for differentiating instruction for students of different levels of experience, the keyboard is an inclusive tool for teaching students with a range of physical abilities as well. Students can perform the role of a keyboard player by using touch screen virtual instruments on an iPad. The smart piano in GarageBand, for example, allows students to perform three- or four-part chords with one finger, by touching the name of the desired chord. Students can also create keyboards by using Makey Makey hardware and software that turns everyday objects, such as Play-Doh and bananas, into keyboard instruments. These devices have been used as accommodations for students who are unable to press the keys of traditional keyboard.

CONCLUSION

Much like the guitar, electric bass, and ukulele, keyboards come in many shapes and sizes. The term keyboard may be applied broadly to a variety of instruments including electric keyboards, MIDI controllers, synthesizers, computer-based or tablet devices, and even acoustic pianos. The variety of keyboard instruments presents many opportunities to popular music teachers and students, with options for differentiation and accommodations to provide inclusive learning experiences. Keyboards can serve many functions in a popular music ensemble, performing melodies, harmonies, chordal accompaniments, bass lines, and even rhythmic accompaniments using percussive sound banks. The keyboard is an essential component in most popular music programs, and is well-suited for instruction across a variety of styles.

Takeaways

- Students can apply the same 1–3–5 root position triad shape to a variety of chords.
- Iconic notation provides instant access to engaging music-making experiences on the keyboard.
- Transposition, backing tracks, and instrument patches are a few of the many beneficial features of electric keyboards.
- Jam Cards and Key Cards allow students to better understand the visual relationships between the keyboard and various chords, harmonic progressions, and scales.

Discussion Questions

1. How does the electric keyboard compare to the acoustic piano?
2. What is the role of a keyboard player in a popular music ensemble?
3. Do you believe iconic notation is an appropriate tool for teaching keyboard students? Why, or why not?
4. What pedagogical approaches mentioned above might you use to teach piano or keyboard to students?

Notes

1 Created by Little Kids Rock, Jam Cards can be downloaded for free at: http://jamzone.littlekidsrock.org/teachers/jam-cards/.
2 Created by Musical Futures International, Key Cards can be downloaded for free at: www.musicalfuturesaustralia.org/.

Drum Kit

The drum kit is one of the most versatile instruments in popular music, used in most genres including rock, pop, metal, and hip hop. Few students (or adults) can resist the temptation to strike a drum when it is within reach and everyone looks instantly cooler seated behind the drum kit. However, it is an instrument that few music teachers play well and relatively few students have an opportunity to learn. Since the drum kit in school music programs is often limited to pep bands and jazz bands (and these ensembles often have one or two drummers), it is no surprise that many music educators do not feel comfortable modeling or teaching drum kit playing in their classrooms. Fortunately, through a simple step-by-step approach to playing drum kit that focuses on accessibility and instant success, music educators of all experience levels can teach this instrument.

BASICS

The drum kit in Figure 7.1 is set up for a right-handed player. Left-handed players will often set up the instrument in reverse order, with the snare drum and hi-hat on the right side of the bass drum and the floor tom on the left side of the bass drum. If you have one drum kit and multiple drummers in each class, we recommend setting the drums up for right-handed players because left-handed students can play on a right-handed setup. The simple truth is the drum kit is a two-handed instrument! The height of the seat (also known as the **throne** or stool) and the height and angle of the drums should all be adjusted to fit the needs of individual students. The drum kit can also be adjusted or broken down into different parts to accommodate students of all abilities. We will discuss opportunities to space out the parts of the drum kit to accommodate multiple players later in this chapter.

Holding the Drumsticks

There are multiple ways to hold the drumsticks. The most common grips in the United States are the American, French, and German grips. They are pretty similar, with some variation on the placement of the thumb and angle of approach when striking the drum. The most important thing for students is a

FIGURE 7.1
Parts of the Drum Kit

FIGURE 7.2
Holding a Drumstick

healthy grip. Each drumstick is held between a curled index finger and thumb at the balanced point so that weight is evenly distributed on both sides of the stick (Figure 7.2). This point is usually about two-thirds of the way from the tip of the drumstick. Vic Firth brand drumsticks have an American Flag at the balanced point of the stick, which is a good starting place for the thumb. The three remaining fingers lightly wrap around the drumstick for stability and support. The stick should rest in the fold of the top knuckle of the pointer figure. For many beginners, the second knuckle is instinctive, but that method of holding the drumstick leads to unhelpful technique down the road. Make sure students do not squeeze the drumstick too tightly because that will limit the bounce of the stick as it rebounds from hitting the drumhead.

Striking the Cymbals and Drums

Most right-handed players will play the hi-hat cymbals with the right hand, the snare drum with the left hand, the bass drum with the right foot, and the hi-hat pedal with the left foot. See Figure 7.1 to identify these parts of the drum kit. Left-handed drummers playing on a right-handed drum kit might find it more comfortable to play the snare drum with their right hand and the hi-hat with their left hand. This technique is called open-handed drumming since the sticks do not cross.

Striking the cymbals in different places and with different parts of the drumstick will change the timbre of the sound considerably (Figure 7.3). A strike to the main part of the cymbal (the **bow**) with the tip of the drumstick produces a lighter, more controlled sound, with a longer sustain. Using the same part of the stick to hit the **bell** of the cymbal (the dome) creates a higher pitch with less sustain. Striking the **rim** (edge) of the crash cymbal with the shoulder or the shaft of the drumstick produces a broader, more aggressive sound. Visit http://popmusicped.com for a link to "One Cymbal, Many Sounds," which demonstrates this concept.

Specific cymbal sounds are appropriate for different styles and contexts. The same is true of drum heads. Striking the snare slightly off-center on the drum head will produce a louder, fuller sound than striking the drum head toward the outside rim of the drum. And striking the drum directly in the center (the node) will cancel out some of the vibration and deaden the sound. The best way to understand the different timbres of the cymbals and drum heads is simply to sit down at a drum kit and explore. By striking the cymbals

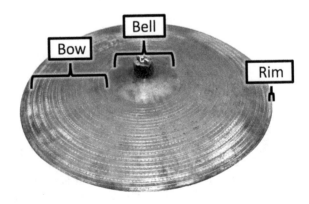

FIGURE 7.3
Striking Surfaces of a Cymbal

and drum heads in different places with different parts of the drumstick, students can discover the many different sonic options available to drummers. For a more detailed exploration of cymbal and drum head striking techniques, check out *Sound Advice for Drummers* by Gareth Dylan Smith.[1]

Drum Kit Notation

Drum kit notation may be expressed using a traditional five-line music staff. Unlike staff notation for pitched instruments, in which the location on the staff indicates a specific pitch, the note placement in drum staff notation corresponds with a drum or cymbal. As shown in Figure 7.4, the percussion clef (also known as neutral clef) is used for nonpitched instruments, such as the drum kit. The clef does not represent all the possible drums or nonpitched percussion instruments that could possibly be notated on the staff; less common instruments (e.g., China cymbal, cowbell) are indicated in the staff with special text and instructions.

Both the Percussion Arts Society and Berklee College of Music's engraving style guides recommend that drum kit instruments played with the hands (e.g., snare drum, cymbals) are notated with an upward-facing stem and instruments played with the feet (e.g., bass drum, hi-hat pedal) are notated with a downward-facing stem. This style makes it easier for drummers to read and perform multiple parts at once.

Figure 7.5 represents a common rhythm in popular music, which includes the **backbeat**. The backbeat, a term used to describe playing the snare drum on beats two and four, is used in countless songs and is the backbone of most popular music drum kit parts. This rock beat is performed by playing the bass drum on beats 1 and 3, the snare drum on beats 2 and 4, and a closed hi-hat in an eighth note pattern for all four beats.

As illustrated in Figure 7.5, the rock beat can be expressed with iconic notation, in which pictorial representations of the drums and cymbals are placed in a grid with subdivisions of the beats underneath the pattern. One

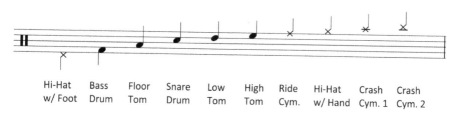

FIGURE 7.4
Drum Staff Notation

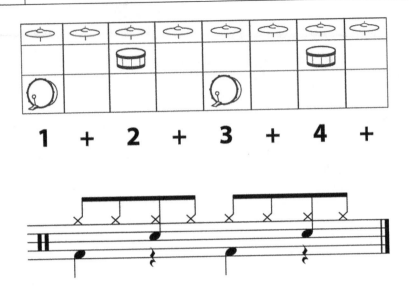

FIGURE 7.5
Staff Notation and Iconic Notation for a Rock Beat Pattern

of the benefits of using iconic notation is that it provides instant access to drum kit patterns. Instead of having to remember that the note on the third space of the percussion clef represents the snare drum, students can easily recognize the picture of the drum or cymbal and immediately know what to play.

APPROACHES

Body Drumming
Body drumming is a great way to introduce the drum kit to students (Figure 7.6). Since it is unlikely (and probably undesired) that you would have a drum kit for each student, having the class start with body percussion familiarizes students with the kinesthetic movements of playing the drum kit.

Getting Started on the Drum Kit
The rock beat comprises three individual parts that must be performed at the same time: the bass drum, the snare drum, and the hi-hat. For a beginning student (or teacher) this can be difficult to do and it may be helpful to divide the drum kit into multiple parts; three people play the rock beat on one drum kit (Figure 7.7).

More students will have the opportunity to play the drum kit by using this approach. While your classroom might have a ukulele or guitar for each

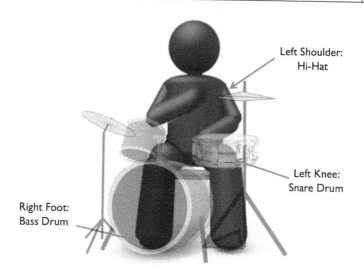

FIGURE 7.6
Body Drumming
Image courtesy of Little Kids Rock

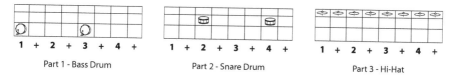

FIGURE 7.7
One Rock Beat Performed by Three Players

student, it likely will not have a drum kit for each student. Allowing multiple students to play the drum kit at the same time increases access to the instrument for all the students in your class. Once students feel comfortable playing the different parts of the drum kit individually, they can start to play multiple parts at the same time. One of the easiest places to start is by having students play the bass drum and snare drum parts together. This can help them begin to understand how to move both their legs and arms to play drum rhythms. While some students will respond well to learning parts individually and then putting it all together, other students will find it easier to learn all of the parts together slowly, so that they can better understand the interdependence of the parts. For more examples of exercises to build limb independence (and limb interdependence) visit http://popmusicped.com.

Variations of the Rock Beat

After students have learned the basic rock beat, they should branch out by trying other drum kit patterns. Here are some common variations of the rock beat that are used in popular music:

Four on the Floor

This groove (Figure 7.8) is similar to the rock beat from Figure 7.5, but includes the hi-hat and bass drum on each of the four beats.

More Rock Beats

This rock beat adds the bass drum on the "and of 3" (Figure 7.9).

Opening the Hi-Hat

Once students can perform the rock beat and some of its variations, they will be ready for the technique of opening and closing the hi-hat. Opening and closing the hi-hat changes the timbre and the dynamics of the sound. This

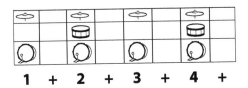

FIGURE 7.8
Four on the Floor

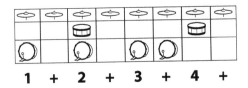

FIGURE 7.9
Bass Drum on "and of Three"

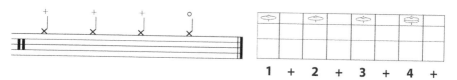

FIGURE 7.10
Staff Notation and Iconic Notation for Closed and Open Hi-Hats

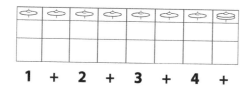

FIGURE 7.11
Practice Activity for a Closed and Open Hi-Hat

timbral difference is often used to create some variety in a repetitive rhythm. In standard drum notation, the open hi-hat is notated with an "o" above the note and a closed hi-hat has a "+" sign. Using iconic notation, you can simply include a photo of the hi-hat in an open position. In Figure 7.10, the first three beats are played with the hi-hat closed and the fourth beat is played with the hi-hat open.

A simple activity to practice the opening of the hi-hat is to isolate the hi-hat part, playing with a closed hi-hat until the "and" of beat 4 (Figure 7.11).

Drum Fills

A drum fill is an improvised or rehearsed pattern that signals the beginning of a new phrase or section. A fill may deviate from the main beat or may be performed in addition to (on top of) the groove. Fills help to break up the monotony of repetitive drum patterns and often happen at the end of a measure or section. One of the most common drum fills is a measure-long fill in which the drummer plays eighth or sixteenth notes on the snare drum, each of the rack toms, and the floor tom (Figure 7.12).

Some drum fills last just one beat, such as the fill in Figure 7.13 which includes sixteenth notes on beat four.

Visit http://popmusicped.com for more examples of drum fills.

Students can also create their own drum fills by playing the rhythm of a spoken phrase on the snare, rack toms, and floor tom. For example, you could ask a

FIGURE 7.12
Sample Drum Fills

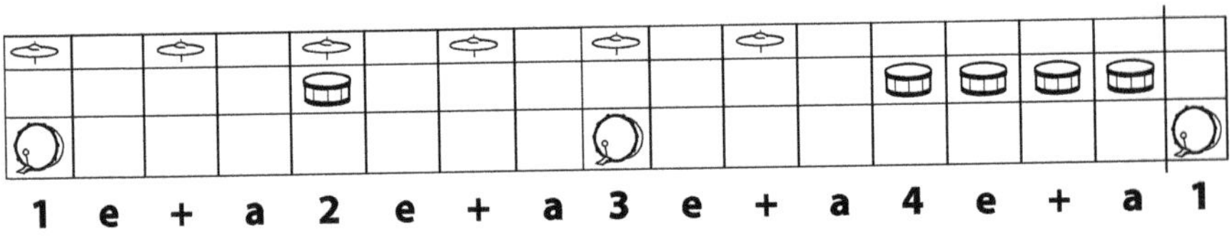

FIGURE 7.13
Drum Fill Lasting One Beat

student to perform their favorite dinner as a drum fill on the instrument after three measures of a backbeat pattern. The student would play time for three measures and then place their response (e.g., turkey with mashed potatoes) on the kit. Students may be more likely to play in time if they speak the phrase out loud as they improvise their fill.

Controlling Volume Levels

One common challenge with playing the drum kit in school classrooms is the sound; drums can be loud! This can be especially problematic if your music room shares a wall with another classroom. Before discussing ways to control the loudness of the drums, it is important to first discuss hearing health. Protecting your students' hearing should be a top priority for all music teachers. Ear plugs should be required for everyone in your popular music ensemble. Not only will this requirement protect their hearing while they are in your class, it will establish good habits for your students for the rest of their lives. With this in mind, there are several different ways to control the sounds that the drum kit makes. Here are a few:

- *Moongel.* An adhesive gel pad that sticks to the surface of drum heads and cymbals to reduce the resonance of the sound.
- *Tape and tissue.* Taping a folded piece of tissue paper on the outside edge of the drum will reduce the resonance and overtones of the drum.
- *Drum mutes.* Rubber pads that lay on top of drum heads and cymbals to dampen the sound.

- *Blankets and pillows.* Putting blankets and/or pillows in your bass drum reduces the resonance of the bass drum and muffles the sound.
- *Practice cymbals.* Cymbals with hundreds of tiny holes to reduce the resonance of the cymbal when it is struck.
- *Multi-rod drumsticks.* These drumsticks are bound dowel rods that produce a softer attack than traditional drumsticks

Electronic Drum Kits

One potential solution for controlling the sound of a drum kit is to use an **electronic drum kit** (EDK). An EDK allows the student or teacher to digitally control the volume with a dial. Additionally, there are many other advantages to using an EDK, including expanding the range of sounds that the drum kit can produce. Most basic EDKs will allow the user to choose various preset sounds such as rock kits, jazz kits, and even hip hop-inspired sounds. The EDK can also make it easier to record the drum kit. Instead of miking the drum kit, you can simply capture the sounds from the control box of the EDK. The electronic control box houses different sound patches and processes each strike of the drum or cymbal. When using an EDK in performance, the recorded "sounds" will be captured as MIDI data, which provides options for editing and **mixing** the recording. For more information about MIDI devices, check out Chapter 10: Digital Audio Workstations. In addition to EDKs, there are many electronic tools that can be used while playing the drums: triggers, sample modules, click-tracks, and various other pieces of hardware. While a full examination of these types of technologies is outside the scope of this chapter (especially since technologies are always changing and evolving), it is worth looking into the latest drum technologies that will allow your students to access more sounds and take their drumming to the next level.

Bucket Drums

Bucket drumming is an affordable way to engage an entire class in drumming activities. Five-gallon buckets are commonly used for this activity; they are inexpensive and can easily be found at local hardware stores. Some hardware stores even donate buckets to local area schools for use in music classrooms. There are different ways to play a bucket drum: (1) strike the center of the bottom of the bucket; (2) strike the rim of the bottom of the bucket; (3) strike the side of the bucket; and (4) click the sticks together. Students can also create their own percussion notation for bucket drumming to write songs. One example of bucket drumming notation is found in Figure 7.14.

Classroom Percussion

Students can reproduce the rock beat using classroom percussion or found objects. In the example in Figure 7.15, maracas replace the hi-hat, rhythm sticks replace the snare drum, and a hand drum replicates the bass drum. Students can explore different timbres of classroom instruments to recreate the rock beat as an accompaniment to popular or folk songs.

Center of Bucket   Edge of Bucket   Stick Click   Side of Bucket

FIGURE 7.14
Bucket Drumming Notation Legend

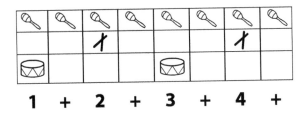

1 + 2 + 3 + 4 +

FIGURE 7.15
Rock Beat Using Classroom Percussion

DIFFERENTIATION

As mentioned previously, challenging drum kit parts may become more access-ible by dividing the instrument into individual parts: hi-hat, snare, toms, and bass drum. As students get more comfortable playing the drums, they will nat-urally try to play multiple parts and will progress at their own speed. Breaking the drum kit down into separate parts can also provide access for students with varying abilities who might not have the capacity to independently move their legs and arms to play certain parts of the instrument. The ubiquity of the rock beat in popular music allows teachers to utilize it for almost any song (most pop songs are in 4/4 meter). For songs that have drum parts that are more difficult to play, the rock beat will still work! Having students start on the rock beat for these songs will allow them to participate right away while they take their time in learning more difficult rhythms.

Students of various physical abilities may also participate by performing the drum kit role on touch screen virtual instruments, such as the drum kit in GarageBand for iOS. Samplers can also replicate any number of percussion instruments and be easily triggered by the touch of a finger or other body part, depending on the mobility and dexterity of the individual student.

CONCLUSION

Every student in a music classroom can participate in drum kit activities, even if no drum kit is available. Through body percussion, bucket drumming, classroom instruments, and creative approaches to breaking the drum kit up into multiple parts, students can learn to perform a rock beat and other rhythm patterns essential to popular music. All students in an ensemble setting can, and should, learn to play a basic rock beat, even if there is a dedicated drummer in the group. By understanding the drum kit and its function in an ensemble or music class, all students will be better able to perform their own individual roles and contribute to the groove more effectively.

Takeaways

- The basic rock beat is easy to learn and works for most popular music songs.
- Provide access and instant success by dividing the drum kit into parts for multiple students.
- EDKs and accessories to dampen the resonance of the drum kit help to keep the volume of the classroom at an appropriate level.

Discussion Questions

1. What are your previous experiences with playing the drum kit (if any)?
2. What are some approaches to teaching the drum kit that you might use in your future classroom?
3. What are some of the challenges of using a drum kit in the classroom and how might you deal with those challenges?
4. How might the drum kit be added to other music ensembles?

Note

1   Smith, *Sound Advice for Drummers.*

Vocals

S inging is a complex art form and there are as many ways to sing as there are genres of music. The skills required to sing various types or styles of music vary greatly, but there are common attributes among all forms that result in sustainable singing. Learning to sing in a way that does not harm the vocal mechanism and contributes positively to lifelong vocal health is essential, especially for children. When younger students can learn to sing popular music styles with good technique endemic to the style in which they are singing, they are more likely to have positive experiences as singers throughout their lives.

Singing is a quintessential element of many genres of music and is often understood to be the primary means of storytelling within songs, which is at the heart of musical communication. The lead singer, as the interpreter of the lyrics, relays the song's story and intention while maintaining the audience's attention. Background singers add harmony and support the lead singer. Whether performing lead or background vocals, a singer can connect to an audience, both sonically and visually, allowing for the amplification of experience. The quality and uniqueness of the singer's voice, coupled with their projected personality, influences the audience's enjoyment of a performance.

Although many music teacher education programs include singing as a technical component of required coursework, not all singing is the same. Popular and classical vocal technique require different preparation and one approach does not automatically equal success in the other. Popular music singing contains distinctive phonological and stylistic elements that require unique approaches and techniques.[1] While the approach to singing and techniques required for improvement may vary between styles,[2] the fundamentals for singing are essential to all vocal techniques regardless of the genre. Despite your own familiarity with popular music singing, elements of good singing are universal enough to lay a foundation of singing in tune while maintaining vocal health.

BASICS

Popular music typically features a forward and bright voice quality that is different from the vocal production of classical singers in terms of coordination of the acoustic setup, breath management, and most importantly registration, especially for female singers, where keys are set typically in the lower octave.[3] Popular music singing utilizes differing attributes of **phonation**, including a higher and narrower **larynx** and a high back of tongue position. It relies on personalized phrasing that is accompanied by a speech-like articulation, is consonant-driven vocal production, and prefers the voicing of diphthongs over the use of pure vowels.[4] Popular music singers often employ limited or no vibrato.

In the past, these differences in vocal production were often viewed as aesthetically inferior,[5] damaging, and flawed by classically minded teachers.[6] However, poor technique when singing in any style can result in vocal injury. Teaching students to have good technique in whatever style they are singing will contribute to their long-term vocal health. Understanding and being able to teach good vocal health in all vocal styles, including popular music styles, can alleviate concerns that music teachers may have about the inclusion of popular music in schools.

While the foundational elements of good singing technique are essential across genres, popular music singing includes defining elements of stylized vocal production, often requiring a complex layering of "effects" specific to the genre. Any or all of these vocal effects can cross style boundaries to be employed by a popular music singer, sometimes even within a single performance. Reflecting on the hybrid nature of popular music and the crossover of style boundaries, some authors in the field of voice science describe a distinctive vocal production that is identifiably different from that of classical singers.[7]

COMMONLY INCLUDED VOCAL EFFECTS BY STYLE[8]

- Rock singing includes growls, glottal onsets, and screams.
- Pop singing includes soft onset, yell, and vocal fry.
- Country singing includes yodeling, crying, and riding an American "r."
- Jazz requires a breathy onset, glottal stroke, and scat.
- Musical theater singing requires character voice, belt, legit (modified classical), and pop/rock elements.

Visit http://popmusicped.com for more information about these techniques.

Popular music singing can be more challenging as a result of audience expectations for a visual performance. No matter how amazing each band member may be, most attention will be directed to the lead singer, as they spend most of their time positioned at center stage. An essential element of lead singing is stage presence, which consists of movement and physical displays of emotional communication. Understanding the lyrics and investing emotionally and physically in presenting them can help to solidify the audience's attention and authenticate popular music singing.

Singing Is Personal

Unlike other instruments, the singing mechanism is located within the physical body. Criticism from others, or from the self, can have long-lasting effects upon the confidence level of a singer. Children label themselves as singers or nonsingers at increasingly younger ages. Media and television shows that promote competition adds to the perception that you either can or cannot sing. However, singing is a learned skill that everyone with a typically developed vocal mechanism can improve. Learning to sing popular music styles with solid technique and healthy habits can lead to an overall improvement in musical growth, self-acceptance, emotional creativity, and even healing.

Teachers, students, and family members may send mixed messages about gender and singing. Singing is frequently perceived as a thing that girls do. However, within the professional music industry, the reality is very much the opposite. While it may appear that female performers have taken over the charts, they remain far behind men in terms of all aspects of performance, producing, and songwriting. Despite the pioneering work of artists such as Janis Joplin, Grace Slick, Tina Turner, Patti Smith, Joan Jett, Chrissie Hynde, and Stevie Nicks, among others from the 1960s onward, more men make music, including singing and rapping on albums, than women. With each passing decade, more women have broken into the popular music industry; however, across the creative roles within professional recording studios, women make up 21.7 percent of artists, 12.3 percent of songwriters, and 2.1 percent of producers. Hip hop, the most popular and growing genre since the year 2000, is 95 percent male in terms of performing artists.[9] While these numbers are discouraging for females and reveal a systematic inequality in the music industry, it may be encouraging to male K-12 students as substantial evidence that singing is for everyone. Popular music in the schools may help tackle these inequalities and lead to a future where more females are making, writing, and producing popular music professionally.

APPROACHES

The implementation of good singing technique can lead to lifelong vocal health and enjoyment. As mentioned previously, good foundational skills can be found across all singing styles. Good singing habits include an understanding and practice of (1) posture, (2) supportive breath, (3) phonation, and (4) **singing range** and **vocal register**. As these basic skills are studied, students can also begin to learn the more advanced skills of **belting** and genre-specific techniques. An understanding of foundational skills should lead to more advanced skills such as changes in phonation, the introduction to belting, and other extended techniques such as scream singing.

> Additional strategies, information, and student exercises for each of these components may be found at http://popmusicped.com.

Posture

Awareness of optimal postural placement increases the likelihood of success while decreasing the potential for injury. Optimal singing posture enables the singer to remain relaxed, thus avoiding physical stresses that can affect vocal health and quality, and provides physical support for breathing and the vocal mechanism. Postural understanding consists of an awareness of the position of the feet, knees, hips, abdomen, chest, shoulders, arms, hands, and head in relationship to each other. Posture is the foundation of powerful and tension-free singing. While standing is an ideal way to support singing, it is not always possible such as when playing an instrument for a singer with differing physical needs. Seated posture can also support good singing if the following areas are considered.

Seated Posture

- Base of the pelvic bones down – when seated properly, the two ends of the pelvic bones will be facing downwards toward the chair. When seated, place your hands below your bottom and slowly rock back and forth. You will feel two bones. When these bones point downwards, it will cause your breathing support system to align vertically, including pelvis, spine, and head. Your chest should feel tall and wide, easily moving in all directions.
- Keep your head aligned with the rest of your body. This can be challenging when playing an instrument. Master your instrument and the songs you are playing to avoid staring at your fingers on a stringed instrument or your hands on the drums or keyboard. When you do need to look down, do so by using the joint between your skull and your spine to tilt your head down without causing the chest to collapse or the spine to curve. Make sure that the microphone is well positioned to allow you to sing directly forward.
- Feet placed about shoulder-width apart on the floor. Slight bend in the knees. Hips situated evenly over the feet and knees – it can help to "feel the heels into the ground" to experience what this balance is like. Shoulders should be in line with the hips and not hunching forward to back, and from there the head should rise neutrally over the shoulders. Jaw is neutral and tongue is relaxed. Eyes are forward – not up or down.

Standing Posture

- *Feet.* Feet should be shoulder-width apart, with one foot slightly in front of the other for balance. The weight of your body should be toward the front of your feet (not on the heels of the feet).
- *Knees.* Knees should remain loose and never locked. Locking knees can result in restricted blood flow and can cause fainting. A good test for keeping the knees loose is to ensure that they can bend or bounce easily.
- *Hips.* Hips should align above your feet and directly below your torso for the maximum amount of support. Some people tend to either rock their hips forward causing a curved torso or to push them back causing increased lower back pain over time.
- *Abdomen.* The abdomen should be flat and firm, held in an easily expandable position.
- *Arms, chest, and shoulders.* Arms and hands can hang loosely at either side of the body, with a little gap between them. Keep your chest high and your shoulders back and down. Shoulders should remain relaxed but tall, allowing for the spine to elongate. If the shoulders are hunched forward, a few shoulder circle-rolls from front to the back, stopping just behind alignment with the torso can be helpful. If the shoulders are pushed back too far from the torso, it can cause stress to both breathing and the vocal mechanism.
- *Head position.* Keep your head level, with the chin parallel to the floor. You may need to adjust your chin back slightly to ensure that the neck is straight. If the chin is pulled up or down it can affect air flow from the abdomen and tightening of the tongue muscles, which can affect sound production.

One way to get students engaged in the many elements that make up good posture is to have them create a rap or rhyming chant consisting of these elements. Here is an example from Paul Reviver Middle School in Los Angeles, CA:

> Shoulders are down, feet firmly on the ground,
> with a slightly bent knee.
> My back is straight to balance my weight,
> My arms are hanging free.
> Lifting up my chest helps me breathe my best.
> Now there's just one last thing.
> Hold my head up right and focus my sight,
> And now I'm ready to sing!

Supportive Breath

Breath control is the ability to regulate the speed and volume of air passed out of the lungs and through the vocal cords. This system involves the **diaphragm** and lungs through the process of inhalation and exhalation. The diaphragm, a dome-shaped muscle below to lungs, controls breathing. During inhalation, the diaphragm contracts, flattens outs, and pulls forward, thus the abdomen should not only expand outward but downward pulling air drawing air into the lungs. During exhalation, the diaphragm relaxes to allow for the movement of air out of the lungs. Deep breathing has little to do with shoulder elevation, and raising the shoulders can work against free singing, as it can cause unwanted tension within the neck and shoulder area. A good breath for singing is low and deep, filling from the bottom of the lungs to the top. Well-trained singers diligently practice breathing techniques in order to increase the amount of air they can inhale and to control the velocity and volume of air they exhale. Mastery of singing long notes and phrases as well as dynamics require expert breath control.

Phonation

Phonation is the physical process by which sound is produced. When the vocal folds are resting (not in the process of producing sound or keeping things out of the airway, such as when eating or drinking) they are open, allowing air easy passage through the larynx into the lungs. When they are vibrating, the opening appears smaller or even closed. During phonation, air is brought into the lungs (through the larynx and past the open vocal folds) from the contraction of the diaphragm. As the diaphragm relaxes, it causes air to move out of the lungs and into the larynx. The larynx is the organ that forms a passage into the lungs. The larynx holds the vocal folds. Vocal folds are membranes stretched across the larynx. Sound is produced from the oscillation of the vocal folds (or vocal cords) and subsequent resonances of the vocal tract. This vibration is referred to as voicing or giving voice.

Vocal Singing Range and Registration

Vocal range is the full set of pitches that someone is physically capable of producing. In terms of vocal range, it does not have to sound pretty to be counted. The range extends from the lowest note a person can sing to highest note they can sing. With training, singers can extend their range both higher and lower over time. **Vocal tessitura,** on the other hand, is the range of notes that are within a comfortable vocal range for a singer and that are the best sounding. Unlike a vocal range, tessitura is not determined by extremes. Within a song, the tessitura is the vocal range in which most of the notes lie. Ideally, a singer is matched to a song that has a similar tessitura to that of their own voice.

While the concepts of range and tessitura are easy to understand, the idea of register is a bit more challenging, particularly in popular music where register is an important characteristic to manipulation of desirable sounds. A vocal register is a specific spectrum of pitches within a singing range that the vocalist can produce at roughly the same quality and in the same way. When switching from one range to the next, a vocalist can often feel a shift in the larynx because the vocal cords vibrate differently. A register break occurs where notes become more difficult to sing as the voice changes from one internal positioning to another. In the classical tradition, singers practice for years to be able to control and blend register changes.

In popular music, all forms of register changes are used depending on the desired sound. Some famous popular music singers, such as Björk, Sinéad O'Connor, and Niall Quinn of the Cranberries, have made a name for themselves by not blending registers and, instead, purposefully causing register breaks for aesthetic appeal. Singers such as Celine Dion, Mariah Carey, Whitney Houston, Sia, and Beyoncé have used register shifts to create large flips and runs between chest voice and head voice, and vice versa. Students learning to sing popular music should be taught to both blend registers and to utilize them in interesting ways.

Classification Of Voice Parts

Knowing each student's voice part (sometimes called range or classification of range) will help you to determine which songs are most appropriate for rehearsing and performance. There are various approaches to determining voice parts and many of these differences are specific to genre, but the tessitura and range are the primary attributes of consideration. Music educators are frequently knowledgeable about classical and operatic voice classifications. Knowing the voice classification in classical music provides us with vocabulary and a structure on which to discuss commonalities and differences (Figure 8.1).

> Visit http://popmusicped.com for a link to vocal ranges of popular musicians.

While knowing the general range of your singers is helpful for selecting songs and transpositions, true classification of voices in popular music is much more challenging than in other styles of singing for several reasons. First, voice categorizations do not always consider unique vocal effects specific to popular music genres. Second, voice classifications were constructed for the grouping of singers found within choir and that are not necessarily a part of common popular music styles. Third, belting includes the use of chest voice higher than is typical in classical singing (more on this later in the chapter). Because of these challenges, voice classification for popular music singing is highly specific. This means that although a singer may have the vocal range to sing a song, they may not be the ideal candidate to do so because of the song or genre's vocal timbre, vocal effects, or register tessitura.

Selecting Music to Match Singing Range

One of the more challenging aspects of selecting repertoire is ensuring that the song's tessitura matches the vocal attributes of the singer and the song's range is within the range of the singer. The easiest way to determine fit is to have the student or students attempt to sing the selected song in the key in which it is written. You can also compare the singer's tessitura with the outer ranges of the melody. If they are not a match, consider transposing the song to a key

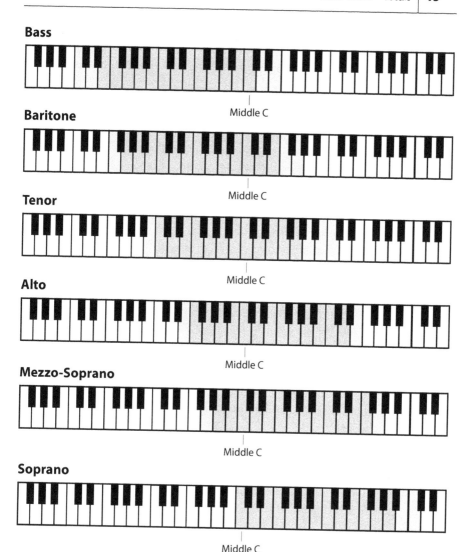

Bass

Middle C

Baritone

Middle C

Tenor

Middle C

Alto

Middle C

Mezzo-Soprano

Middle C

Soprano

Middle C

FIGURE 8.1
Vocal Ranges

that works well for the singer. Take into consideration how a transposition would affect the instrumental parts and players. If transposing to a different key is not in the band's best interest, you may need to switch to a different lead singer or select a different song. Sometimes transposing the key of a song helps everyone, including instrumentalists, and the former lead singer may transition to a back-up singer, creating interesting harmonies for the song that fits their voice well.

Sometimes you find a song that is almost perfect. Here are some strategies to make those songs work.

- When transposing a song typically performed by a tenor to fit a treble voice, it is not uncommon for the chorus to be in the high or too high range for the singer. Consider flipping the chorus an octave lower than is typical. On many songs the audience will not even notice. Another solution is to have different signers for the verse and the chorus, selecting someone with a higher range for the chorus.
- Some of the most challenging elements of a song are not part of the melody and, instead, are vocal variations or improvisations. Embracing approximation, consider eliminating, simplifying, or rewriting any variations to the melody that go beyond the singer's range or tessitura.
- Do not forget the capo! Singers who play guitar or ukulele can use a capo to easily change the key without having to learn or utilize new chords. Singers who play keyboard can use a transpose button to change the key of a song as well.

Belting

Belting is one of the most utilized techniques in musical theater and popular music styles. There are many different approaches and techniques for belting.[10] Physiologically, when a singer is belting, the vocal folds visibly shorten and thicken, while they undulate along more of their vertical surface area. In terms of phonation, in belting the vocal folds are together for more time during each vibratory cycle. Because of this, there are slight changes to airflow as less air is escaping during each cycle. Acoustically, belting uses different acoustic tuning strategies, meaning the harmonics utilized to create in-tune singing are different based on vowels and where the pitch is within a given range.[11]

Belting often produces a sound that is bright, loud, and contains multiple formants so as to resonate and be perceived as loud. It is similar to a call or shout with sustained pitch and, sometimes, vibrato.[12] Belting has a unique physical quality that can often be felt in the chest. If done incorrectly over longer periods of time, belting can cause damage to the vocal folds (as any singing can without proper technique). However, when done correctly, belting can add a heightened sense of emotion to music.

In these exercises you will feel the changes that your body experiences when belting.

Exercise: The Lost Phone[13]

Your chest and upper body are where the physical elements of belting are often felt, but all sound emanating from the voice that is made by humans originates at the level of the vocal folds. To explore where belting is often felt in the body, imagine you have just witnessed a person leaving their phone at the register of the store and heading toward the door.

1.   Using a loud voice, put up your hand and yell "Hey" in a firm voice. Pay attention to the feeling of expansion within your chest.
2.   Do the same exercise again but place your hands on the side of your rib cage and feel the expansion as you say "Hey" or "Wait."
3.   Call out again but hold each "Hey" or "Wait" for five seconds or more, and examine and analyze the feeling of the sustained shout.
4.   Call out again but raise the pitch of the "Hey" or "Wait" until you reach the top of your range. Examine and analyze the physical feelings of bringing the calling or shouting elements into your higher range. This exercise can be done near a piano to determine the highest comfortable pitch the calling out can be brought up to. This will help you to understand your current belting range.

In popular music, most singers perform as a soloist or in small groups. This means that music educators need to adapt and utilize techniques that may be similar to what is experienced in private lessons into a classroom environment. This requires adjusting teaching techniques to instruct a large group at one time. Much of the basics of belting should be approached in a manner similar to the ways in which vocal warmups occur in a choral classroom. They should be specific and purposeful in their intent to teach new skills. We suggest that the practice of belting be a part of daily vocal warmups in the popular music classroom. The mixed speech exercises below are a wonderful way to quickly work on these skills as a large group. These exercises can be adapted to fit the age level and interest level of the students.

MIXED SPEECH SOUNDS: SUGGESTED ACTIVITIES

Singers who can belt well often mix speech with singing. This is done by controlling the soft palate, which is located above the tongue and toward the back of the mouth. The following exercises created by Mary Saunders-Barton allow the singer to feel the raising of the soft palate and to begin exploration of mixing singing and speech qualities.[14] Visit http://popmusicped.com for recorded samples of these exercises.

Soft Palate Awareness and Control

To develop soft palate movement, try the following:

Panting (like a dog) with the tongue extended.
Incipient (the beginning of) a sneeze (AH ... AHHH) with no "choo."
Incipient yawn with mouth closed.
Incipient swallow with no gulp.

Phrases for Mixing Speech Voice and Singing Voice

Using as much range as possible, practice mixing speech and singing elements together with the following phrases. For treble voices, try a range from C4 to E5 as is appropriate for age.

> Oh, no you don't!
> May I come in? (Try it with a British accent.)
> No way!
> Never, never, no!
> Where are you going! (Accusatory.)
> Holy cow!
> Yikes!
> Wowie!
> Hey guys!
> I can't go!
> How are you?
> Let me go!
> Hello!

Speaking to Singing

Try the exercises in Figure 8.2 to mix speech and singing together at specific pitch. These exercises move from lower to upper registers, which is more comfortable for those new to belting, and upper down to lower registers, which is a more advanced skill.

Scream Singing

It is next to impossible for a heavy metal screamer to be able to use their voice in a legitimate singing manner after the wear and tear on the vocal cords caused by true screaming has occurred. It is highly recommended that young singers avoid **scream singing** and that teachers discourage this approach until the singer is old enough to make decisions about their own vocal health. When choosing a potentially damaging vocal style, singers may like "singing" in this manner now, but it may have long-lasting consequences that affect their ability to use their voice in a balanced manner in the future.

To simulate screaming, many good rock artists use the microphone to great effect. For example, a very soft cry type of sound highly amplified (mouth close to the mic) can sound like a scream without changing good vocal technique. Vocalists can also take advantage of many distortion effects that guitarists use. Connecting a pedal to a vocal mic can expand the amount of potential distortion and give a much edgier scream sound than a singer could ever accomplish on their own. Another adaptation to avoid screaming is to simply have the singer sing the parts that are typically screamed. In many songs, the audience will not notice or care about the difference.

SINGING EXERCISES

FIGURE 8.2
Speaking to Singing Exercise

INTONATION

Intonation can be defined simply as the rise and fall of the voice, but most often the term is used to describe the accuracy of the voice in matching pitch. Intonation is primarily a matter of pitch variation produced by a complex combination of variables including breath support, vibrato, placement, and other physiological attributes. Recent research in music education that have investigated vocal intonation and pitch accuracy has focused on the amount and quality of vocal training, maturation, and task difficulty on children's singing accuracy[15] and use of singing voice.[16] It is important to be aware that functions attributed to intonation, such as the expression of emotion or highlighting aspects of the lyrics, almost always involve a complex mixture of attributes and that intonation is not a single system of contours and levels but the interaction of various phonological systems including tone, pitch-range, volume, rhythm, and tempo.

Many people assume that poor intonation is the result of singers not hearing or perceiving the pitch correctly. Singers can find it difficult to recognize when they are out of tune because what they "hear" is not the sound that the audience hears due to directionality of sound and internal process of phonation. While debate remains on whether pitch inaccuracy is a matter of perception, many intonation issues can be corrected by focusing on good technique for sound production. Telling singers that they are out of tune or "pitchy" may help them to recognize there is an issue, but it does nothing to assist them in correcting it and many young singers will not know how to fix the problem. All aspects of vocal technique as discussed above (posture, breath support, resonance, jaw and tongue position, vowels, consonants, vibrato, etc.) contribute to intonation accuracy or inaccuracy.

In order to understand the basic cause of a singer's pitch inaccuracy it may be helpful to consider personal attributes of singing. These are elements that are completely at the control of the singer and are related to good singing technique. Julia Davids and Stephen LaTour, authors of the online text *Vocal Technique*,[17] suggest that when working with an inaccurate singer a teacher must consider the common challenges of incorrect intervals, too much or too little breath pressure, inappropriate resonance space, and tension.

- *Incorrect perception of intervals or mode.* Singers must accurately perceive the space or distance between notes, otherwise known as intervals. Knowing the distance between pitches can dramatically improve pitch accuracy. Part of interval training should include experiences in a variety of modes. Even young singers should be able to identify the mode in which they are singing in order to develop expectations for intervals they may encounter. They should also have a general understanding of their own singing range and where the melody they are singing resides within their range. While most singers may be in tune within a portion of the singing range, inexperienced singers can struggle to maintain intonation in specific passages. Two typically challenging areas include register changes and the lowermost or uppermost areas of the singer's range. In addition, they need to develop muscle memory for the correct distance between intervals. Pitches and melodies learned incorrectly become a part of muscle memory and are difficult to correct later.

- *Too much or too little breath pressure.* Too little breath pressure on a given pitch will cause the pitch to be flat and too much breath pressure will cause it to go sharp. In general, as pitch ascends, more breath pressure is needed. Pitch can also be affected by a singer's anxiety or nervousness, both of which can compromise breath control.
- *Insufficient or incorrect resonance space.* A lack of sufficient resonance space can cause a singer to sound flat. Additionally, if the jaw and tongue are in an incorrect position for the vowel being sung, intonation will be compromised.
- *Excessive tension in the neck, larynx, or tongue.* Tension causes problems with intonation as it affects resonance space and the singer's ability to create correct breath pressure. Poor posture and incorrect approaches to breathing are major causes of tension.

Voice Change and Intonation

Intonation difficulties may also be a result of maturation and voice changes that accompany adolescence. Adolescence is the traditional phase of growth between childhood and adulthood that typically takes place between the ages of 10 and 23 years old. During this time, both male and female voices will change and mature. Within adolescence, the biggest vocal changes occur during puberty, especially in young men. During puberty, the male hormone testosterone causes many significant changes, including faster growth of the larynx along with increases in the size and thickness of the vocal folds. Having longer folds decreases the frequency fundamental for males and the thicker folds produce a register change resulting in a change in the quality or timbre of the voice. Voice changes in pubescent males can vary widely between young men, thus only general statements may be made. For example, a full class of seventh-grade boys may likely represent all stages of voice maturation. Typical adolescent boys' voices often begin to mutate at 12–13 years of age with an evening out of the changes between the ages of 15 and 18 years. During this time, lower pitches tend to be more stable than upper pitch ranges. Most of the active changes tend to occur within one year of when the initial attributes begin to appear.

Female voice changes are often less obvious than that of males but tend to exhibit increased breathiness or huskiness, occasional "cracking," a lowering of average speaking fundamental frequency, and decreased pitch accuracy while singing. The physiologic components that account for female voice changes include facial development that affects voice resonance, a descent of the larynx and equally a lengthening the vocal tract, and increased circumference of chest wall and lung providing greater breathing capacity. While some young females may not notice much of a change, others may struggle with intonation and vocal timbre.

Voice change can also occur when a singer is experiencing gender transition. Transgender singers have specific needs in the development of voice pedagogy that should be informed by cultural competence and an understanding to the social, emotional, physical, and physiological challenges of transition.[18] Because many of the current systems in place for learning how to sing are so firmly anchored in gender binary systems, the singing life of a transgender or nonbinary student can be overwhelmingly stressful and they are often forced into groups in which they feel they don't belong. There are a growing number of resources specific to the transgender voice and these can be found on the companion website. Visit http:// popmusicped.com for more information about these techniques.

OUT-OF-TUNE SINGERS

To assist singers who are struggling with intonation try the following techniques:

- Place singers who are struggling with intonation (for any reason) alongside the stronger singers within the group. Singing next to strong singers will help them to utilize their listening skills to emulate the sounds around them.
- Instead of asking students to find your starting pitch, take a moment to find their staring pitch. If a student repeatedly enters the song at a lower or higher pitch, it may be that the song selected is not in the best key for their voice. Consider what it might take to transpose the song into the best key for the singer. If transposition causes too many challenges for the rest of the band, consider a different lead singer for that song or, perhaps, striking the song from the set all together. Another option may be to move the singer to the role of back-up singer, and have them add harmony to the melody in a range that is most appropriate for their voice.
- Sometimes singers have a difficult time hearing their own voice within a band. Consider increasing the amplification of the voice microphone and be sure to use a monitor that is facing the band so that they can best hear themselves.
- To increase the singer's ability to hear themselves, consider using personal amplification. The simplest form of this is to have the singer place the palm of their hand in front of but not touch their mouth with the fingers of that hand pointing back toward their own ear. This allows for light amplification of their own sound. You can also create inexpensive amplifiers by using PVC piping and joints to create the receiver on an old-fashioned telephone that the singer can hold to their mouth and ear to hear themselves better.
- It is common for singers to have areas of their voice that they feel most comfortable singing in and areas that they do not. Good singing requires strong technical skills and singers should be encouraged to consistently work on transitioning between ranges, including using proper breath support and pressure and maintaining a tension-free vocal mechanism throughout their range. Be on the lookout for physical signs of vocal stress, particularly in

higher ranges, and immediately provide positive and healthy approaches to singing.

- The best model for humans to match vocal pitch to is another voice. While it is tempting to play melodies on keyboard or guitar, if a student is struggling to find the melody or match pitch, consider modeling the vocal line by singing it yourself or having another singer in the class sing it.
- The visualization of intonation is a strong way in which to help out-of-tune singers recognize when they are on and off the pitch. Many modern music video games such as those based on karaoke or playing in bands have the capability of showing (and scoring) singing by indicating how accurate the singing is and when the singer is and is not on pitch. Consider using these games with singers that cannot determine if they are above or below pitch.

What not to do:

- Do not bring direct attention to intonation problems in front of other band members unless you know the singer can handle it and you can offer strong suggestions to remedy the problems they are encountering. Just telling a young or inexperienced singer that they are out of tune does not improve anything and can add unnecessary anxiety and tension, resulting in additional intonation problems.
- While you will likely have some students more interested in singing than others, do not permanently assign students to be singers and nonsingers. Everyone should receive singing instruction and be expected to share their singing voice within the band as a lead or back-up singer.
- Do not encourage poor vocal technique to achieve a certain vocal sound or style. Vocal injuries can affect singers at any age and learning to sing incorrectly can lead to serious, career-ending injuries over time.

Singing in Harmony

Harmony, quite simply, is what you hear when two or more notes are sung together. While the melody of a song typically comes from the underlying harmonic structure of the song, harmony is produced by the selection of another note from that harmonic structure that is not already taken by the melody. Be fierce and fearless! Experimenting with harmonies can be quite challenging at times and mistakes will be made. Encourage a supportive and nonjudgmental environment in which students feel comfortable trying out their ideas.

TIPS FOR SINGING IN HARMONY

- One of the best ways to learn to sing harmony is to sing along with your favorite songs. Once you know the song well, it becomes easier to differentiate between the melody and the harmony.

- Listen and sing along with songs that have simple harmonies. A lot of the doo-wop music of the 1950s and early 1960s has tight harmonies based around singing a third above or below the melody.
- Utilize your music theory chords by playing popular chord progressions such as I–V–vi–IV and sing through on the root, then the third, then the fifth.
- Treat the harmony as a melody. When learning a new harmony, practice it alone without the melody until it feels like it is its own melody, then sing it against the real melody.
- Once a harmony is learned, practice singing it against the melody with your singing partner. Consider slowing the tempo to build confidence in the harmonic structure.
- Often one of the hardest parts about singing harmony is finding the starting note. Use the accompanying chords that play right before the entrance of the harmony part to find the starting note, and practice until it becomes comfortable.
- Sing a well-known song such as "Mary Had a Little Lamb" and then sing it again a third above the melody.
- Record vocal harmonies using a multitrack recording program (see Chapters 9 and 10). Students can experiment with adding harmonies in groups or as individuals.

Learning to sing in harmony can also start with a simple triad and some basic exercises. Select a triad in an appropriate key for the singers. For treble voices, a root of D is often appropriate and for lower voices F is often appropriate. Here are some tips for working with harmonies.

1. Play the major triad on the keyboard and ask the singers to sing the root note on a neutral syllable such as Ah or Oh.
2. Split the group into parts and have some singers retain the root pitch while the other singers sing the major third above it. Switch groups and try this again.
3. Once singing a major third against the root is accomplished, have one group maintain the root while the other group sings a fifth above it. Switch parts.
4. Divide the group into three parts with each group singing either the root, the major third, or the fifth at the same time. Once this is mastered, have students rotate through the root, third, and fifth on command so that one group is always singing each note.
5. Repeat the exercise in a variety of modes including minor. Have students experiment by adding notes beyond the triad and discussing when those harmonies might be appropriate to use in a song.

Singing while playing an instrument is another skill that can be quite challenging. Whether the lead singer or back-up, singing and playing at the same time takes practice and the development of a unique skill set. Here are some tips to help beginners learn to sing and play.

1. Go online and select a song that is relatively easy for the student to play. Print out a chord sheet that contains the lyrics for the song. Then have the student listen to that song with the sheet in hand, pay close attention to when the chords change, and identify where the chords change in accordance to the lyrics.
2. Have the student pick up their instrument and sing the melody while playing the chord changes. The idea is to get comfortable changing chords while they are singing.
3. Once the student can do this consistently, have them add a simple yet consistent pattern under their singing with the chord changes. Begin to alternate the pattern to different, more complex patterns.

VOCAL INJURY

Vocal injuries can have lifelong implications. Your role as a teacher is to listen carefully for not only technique-related issues but for potential vocal problems and injuries. The generic term "dysphonia" encompasses the auditory-perceptual symptoms of voice disorders and is characterized by altered vocal quality, pitch, loudness, or vocal effort. The auditory perception quality of voice in individuals with voice disorders can vary depending on the type and severity of disorder, the size and site of lesion or nodule (if present), and the individual's compensatory responses. The severity of the voice disorder cannot always be determined by the auditory perception of the voice quality alone.

> Visit http://popmusicped.com for additional information about the signs and symptoms of dysphonia and vocal injury.

If a vocal injury is suspected, the singer should be formally assessed by an ENT doctor or otolaryngologist. A request for assessment may be triggered by concerns from individuals, parents, teachers, or health care providers. If you as the teacher suspect a voice disorder, advise the singer to seek an assessment with a medical professional. In a school setting this may be initiated with the school's speech and hearing teacher, but it is recommended that the teacher be in direct communication with the student's family about the concerns and be able to provide evidence from the lists. It should be stressed that you are not a medical professional, but that you are concerned for the student's well-being.

A comprehensive assessment is conducted for individuals suspected of having a voice disorder, using both standardized and nonstandardized measures in which norms are based on age, gender, type of instrumentation used, cultural background, and dialect. Diagnostic therapy may be performed as part of the comprehensive assessment to help in making a diagnosis and to determine whether voice therapy efforts may work for the student. If a formal medical diagnosis is made, the teacher should work in coordination with medical professionals to ensure the singer's needs are being met within the music classroom.

DIFFERENTIATION

Singing is an excellent opportunity for differentiation in popular music classes and ensembles. Unlike all other instruments, everyone in your classes most likely has previous experiences with singing. This does not mean that everyone is good at singing or excited to do it. Singing skills can be developed through regular and purposefully constructed lessons about singing. Having the whole class participate in vocal warmups will go a long way in improving everyone's singing ability. Just as no one should be discouraged from developing skills on instruments, no one should be discouraged from singing. Helping students gain facility and technique in singing can also help them gain confidence and joy when making music with their voices.

Tips to encourage everyone to sing:

- Make group singing an expected part of the opening routine in every class meeting.
- Lower the risk for those who are timid to sing by having all students sing warmups or vocal techniques together. Over time, these groups can become smaller. Do not call on individuals to sing unless you have purposefully built an environment that supports this.
- Sometimes it is easier for people to sing when they are also moving. Engaging in a kinesthetic, full body movement can distract students from being self-conscious about their singing voice as they think about what their bodies are doing.
- Place stronger singers near more challenged singers as it will help them both improve their singing skills.
- If the song is in a difficult key or range for a lead singer, consider transposing it to a better key. If that creates challenges for the instrumentalist, then maybe this is not the best song for that particular lead singer. They can be encouraged to move to a harmony part and sing lead on another song.
- Build in expectations that all group members join the harmony on at least one song. If the singer struggles with intonation or maintaining pitch, see the intonation section above or add a second back-up singer on those parts. Singing out of tune should not be an excuse to not have to work on those skills.
- Encourage students who are playing their instruments well and who are ready for a challenge to try back-up or lead singing while playing. There are tips at http://popmusicped.com on how to help students learn to do this.

CONCLUSION

Singing in popular music styles is an exciting and complex part of many popular music performances. Lead singers are often the storyteller of the band and share the meanings of the lyrics with the audience through their voices and their bodies. Lead singing can be considered both sonic and visual. Popular music singing shares some common foundational skills with more traditional forms of in-school singing, such as choral singing. These common elements include posture, breathing, and phonation. Popular music contains additional required singing skills such as the ability to belt or purposefully manipulate register breaks. Belting is a learned skill that takes time and dedication to develop. Some vocal sounds and techniques, such as scream singing, may be best left until the singer is old enough to make decisions about their own vocal health.

A singer's range and tessitura can help the teacher determine who may be the best fit as the lead singer of a particular song, or may help them to guide students in selecting songs that best fit the vocal ranges of their band. If a singer's range does not fit a song, consider changing the key of the song (ensuring it still works for the instrumentalists) or having the lead singer move to a back-up singing part where they can harmonize around the melody. Problems with intonation could be a result of maturation, difficulty perceiving of pitch differences, or difficulties producing pitch. Harmony is an enjoyable and important part of many genres. While singing harmony in triads is common, pushing singers to find unusual yet complementary harmonies can stretch their musical understanding.

Teachers should always be on the lookout for students who may be experiencing vocal injury. These injuries may present themselves as an increased effort in speaking, frequent coughing, and variable vocal quality throughout the day. In cases where vocal injury is suspected, the music teacher should work with other specialists in the school to have the student tested.

Takeaways

- Singing is a skill that nearly everyone can learn and become good at. Singing well provides a lifelong skill that can promote participation in music far beyond the classroom and formal schooling.
- During live performances, singing is often as much a visual contribution to a band as it is a sonic one. Singers must often work to tell the story of the music through their bodies and facial expressions.
- Breathing is an important element in singing. The exhalation of breath aides in controlling the quality of the sound and the volume, and partially controls the pitch and the tone.
- Belting is a popular technique that mixes upper and lower registers. Through proper technique, it can be done safely. When done well it can add a unique, emotional value to the music. Scream singing is, in general, an unsafe vocal technique that can lead to long-term damage. The screaming effect is better accomplished through the manipulation of amplification.

- There is an incredible joy in singing in harmony with others. Singing in harmony is a basic vocal skill that should be encouraged at all levels from novice to professional singers. Harmonies can be as basic as thirds or as complicated as unique melodies.

Discussion Questions

1. Should all students be encouraged to sing in a school music program?
2. What do you feel are the essential elements or characteristics of a strong lead singer?
3. How might you explain belting as a healthy practice to your local school choir director?
4. How does knowing a singer's range and tessitura assist in song selection?
5. What suggestions can you provide to singers for applying techniques learned through exercises to the songs they sing?
6. What are a few strategies for assisting instrumentalists to practice singing while playing?
7. What should you do if you feel a student may have a vocal injury?

Notes

1 American Academy of Teachers of Singing, "Contemporary Commercial Music Voice Pedagogy," 7–10.
2 Soto-Morettini, *Popular Singing and Style.*
3 Bartlett, "Tailored Training for Contemporary Commercial Singers," 227–43; lower range is being defined as over a range of F3–C5 and up to E♭5.
4 Bartlett, "Reflections on Contemporary Commercial Singing," 27–35.
5 Edwin, "Belting," 67–68.
6 Spivey, "Music Theatre Singing," 607–11.
7 Burns, "Acoustical Analysis of Voice Differences," 549–54; Radinoff, "Vocal Styles and Techniques," 51–59; Thalen and Sundberg, "Describing Different Styles of Singing," 82–93; and Björkner, "Musical Theatre and Opera Singing," 533–40; and Harris, "Emic/Etic Distinction," 329–50.
8 Bartlett, "Reflections on Contemporary Commercial Singing," 27–35.
9 Kelley, Caitlin. "The Music Industry Still Has a Long Way to Go for Gender Equality."
10 For a detailed description of the belting technique, see LeBorgne and Rosenberg, *The Vocal Athlete.*
11 Harrell, "Physiological Differences."
12 Soto-Morettini, *Popular Singing and Style.*
13 Adapted from techniques suggested by Soto-Morettini.
14 Saunders-Barton, "Bel Canto/Can Belto."
15 Demorest and Clements, "Pitch Matching of Junior High Boys," 190–203; Nichols, "Children's Singing Accuracy," 309–21; and Welch et al., "National Singing Programme," 1–22.
16 Rutkowski and Snell Miller, "Effect of Teacher Feedback and Modeling," 1–10.
17 Davids and LaTour, "Singing in Tune."
18 Hearns and Kremer, *Transgender Voices.*

PART II

Music Technology

OBJECTIVES

- **Identify** a variety of apps and software programs that align with teaching and learning objectives.
- **Describe** approaches to teaching music technology in a variety of classroom spaces on a wide range of budgets.
- **Explain** the functions and purposes of digital audio workstations (DAWs) in school music.
- **Evaluate** technologies based on an individual set of criteria (cost, ease of use, location, purpose) to determine optimal tools for (future) students.

Apps and Software

In 1965, Intel cofounder Gordon Moore observed that transistors – components in chip-based technology (e.g., phones, tablets, and computers) – were shrinking at a remarkable rate. Moore predicted the number of transistors that could fit into a single chip would double while costs were reduced by 50 percent, meaning that devices could become half as expensive and twice as powerful every year.[1] This prediction became known as "Moore's Law" and it has generally held true for 50 years as mobile technology rapidly developed. An exponential growth of software capabilities corresponded with this development, including music-related apps and software that have provided teachers and students with new opportunities for music production, collaboration, performance, learning, and assessment.

We live in an era in which many children have access – literally at their fingertips – to a variety of technology-based instruments, recording devices, and instructional tools. Instruments and technologies that sold for thousands of dollars just decades ago are available today for little or no cost. And while economic barriers to music education are very real and concerning, the first national survey of lower-income families on issues related to digital connectivity found that 85 percent of families in the United States living below the federal poverty line have some kind of digital device, smartphone, or tablet, in their household.[2] Many schools are also adopting tablet carts and 1:1 device programs in addition to computer labs to make mobile technology and digital devices more accessible to students. The landscape of music technology is ever-changing, as developers produce and release new music-making tools at a rapid rate. Because of these changes, it is increasingly important for music educators to focus on the pedagogical approaches to teaching with technology, and not worry as much about becoming an expert in any single app or software program. With that in mind, the focus of this chapter is on the practical application of the tools in a music classroom, not the tools themselves.

BASICS

While "app" is an abbreviation for "application," which can be used on any piece of hardware, the term typically refers to programs on mobile devices such as smartphones and tablets. The term "software" is most often used to describe computer programs. Both may exist as a downloaded tool on a device or online in the **cloud**. Cloud-based programs may be accessed from any device connected to the internet, provided it is compatible with the app or software application. Some of the most commonly used devices in schools include tablets, Chromebooks, and computers. Chromebooks primarily run programs that are cloud-based, apps are most common on tablets, and computers may be used to easily access both software applications and cloud-based programs. When determining the most appropriate devices for your school music program, you might consider cost, location, ease of use, and purpose.

Cost

There are many free or low-cost applications that students can use to compose, produce, and perform music. One of the most popular programs is GarageBand, which is free for iOS (mobile) and MacOS (desktop) platforms. Similar DAW programs such as Audacity, BandLab, and Soundation are free and compatible with multiple operating systems. While apps and software may be free or inexpensive, sometimes the devices used to run them are quite expensive. Music teachers could utilize the school's computer lab or Chromebook carts, requiring no additional technology costs if music-specific technology resources were not available. If there were a larger budget for apps and software, through the school or external funding, then more expensive software packages such as Logic and Pro Tools offer students an experience with industry-standard tools for music production, though GarageBand is more than sufficient for most classrooms.

Location

The location of a class may determine which apps and software are most appropriate for that setting. If the class is in a computer lab, then individual stations running free or low-cost DAWs, notation software packages, and other music apps, could work well. If the class meets in a recording studio or classroom with a single computer, then it may be worthwhile to purchase a more advanced, and therefore expensive, DAW, computer, and mixing desk. If the technology is located on a cart, then it makes most sense to purchase the corresponding cloud-based or mobile apps that are compatible with the devices. Music apps are abundantly available for all devices, so it is usually possible to work within the parameters of your school's technology without needing to purchase additional equipment.

Ease of Use

Keep in mind that more expensive programs often offer more options. Advanced tools work well for experienced students in upper level classes but may be overwhelming for a novice. Free apps tend to be user-friendly and serve as a foundation for more advanced technologies. Your own level of comfort with these programs should inform your choice in software and apps. If you are just beginning with specific apps, it will make the most sense to begin with a free software program that may have limited features. As your own experience and comfort level grows, consider exploring more advanced options that may be more authentic to a professional industry setting.

Purpose

Before selecting apps and software programs for a class, it is essential to consider what you want students to be able to do or produce with the technology. The technology should serve as a mechanism by which to meet your class objectives, not the other way around. Also, avoid the pitfall of using technology as a hook or a fun activity to increase student interest as the "fun effect" is usually short-term and does not lead to long-lasting, meaningful engagement. Students will have a deeper level of enjoyment working with music apps and software if they understand how the tool will help them realize their musical goals, so those must be clear and made first.

APPROACHES

In this section, we will explore learning experiences that may be possible with a variety of apps and software programs. These include music production, performance, and learning and assessment activities. The focus of this section is on the application of these technologies, not the specific apps and software tools that may be used.

Music Production (Creating and Arranging Music)

Perhaps the most common use of music apps and software is to create original music. Composition, songwriting, beat-making, and loop-based arrangements are all activities that connect to the *creating* process guiding many of the National Core Arts Standards for Music Education.[3] These experiences also provide students with an opportunity to produce music that is meaningful and relevant to their individual lives. Software-based notation tools (e.g., Sibelius and Finale) and cloud-based notation tools (e.g., Noteflight and Musescore) vary by price and functionality, with the more expensive versions offering more features that may not be necessary to meet your teaching and learning objectives. Cloud-based tools have the advantage of allowing the teacher to create an online worksheet or template for students to complete, and work may be easily shared in online communities. When teaching popular music, however, it is important to remember the benefits and values of creative music tools that do not require an understanding of traditional five-line staff notation. DAWs include software programs such as Audacity, Mixcraft, and GarageBand; cloud-based software such as Soundation, BandLab and Soundtrap; and apps such as GarageBand iOS.

   Students have a great deal of autonomy and choice when creating music with a DAW. The teacher should facilitate the learning process, providing feedback along the way while ensuring access to resources the student may need to meet their goals for the project. Creative production assignments may be completed by individual students or through collaborations with peers, other classes, or partnering schools. Through file-sharing technologies, students may share session files, tracks, production notes, charts, and other documents related to the production of original music with their collaborators. Sharing protocols that allow students to present their work and comment on the work of their classmates will encourage dialogue and foster community in the classroom. These sharing practices may lead to new understandings as students identify desirable approaches and techniques demonstrated by their peers that may be incorporated into their projects. Online services such as JamKazam and Bandmix may extend these collaborations by providing a space to rehearse, perform, and record music online with musical partners.

◣ MULTI-SELFING ACTIVITIES

Any of the previously mentioned DAWs and some video-based apps (e.g., acapella) allow users to record layers of tracks. Music education scholar Radio Cremata describes how students can engage in "multi-selfing" activities that replicate the performer through multiple audio and/or video recordings;[4] many schools and individual students created multi-selfing projects during the COVID-19 pandemic. Visit http://popmusicped.com for links to engage students in multi-selfing activities using audio/video multitrack recording apps and software.

Performance

Music education professor David Williams facilitates an iPad ensemble at the University of South Florida. The ensemble uses apps to perform a wide variety of songs and styles, including original music written specifically for the iPad.[5] In his article titled "The iPad is a Real Musical Instrument," Williams argues that the iPad shares commonalities with acoustic instruments – it requires practice, it has limitations, it can sound beautiful or bad, it requires a person to touch it, and it is the individual human who possesses the musicianship, creativity, and imagination to make the instrument (whether it be an iPad or an oboe) sound musical.[6]

Other instruments are also dependent upon software for live performance use. Ableton Push is a controller that integrates with Ableton Live, a DAW software program for MacOS and Windows. The Push has a colorful display of touch-sensitive pads that trigger sounds and loops when pressed. It contains a variety of buttons, navigation controls, dials, and a touch strip that controls different parameters of the performance. Much like any other instrument, a musician performing on a Push device with Ableton Live software must develop technique through many hours of practice. The device may be used to create original music, make beats, perform melodies and harmonies,

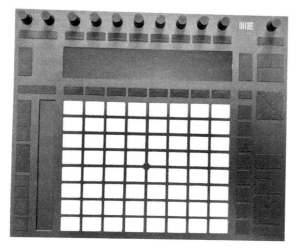

FIGURE 9.1
Ableton Push 2

and produce samples of other sound sources. Visit http://popmusicped.com for a video link to a demonstration of the Ableton Push (Figure 9.1).

Some schools and universities are experimenting with combinations of acoustic, electronic, and computer-based instruments into a single small group ensemble. Music education professor Jonathan Kladder developed a course titled *Hybrid Ensembles in Public Schools*, which challenges students to create original music or recreate cover songs using a combination of woodwind, brass, percussion, and digital instruments. Kladder defines a hybrid ensemble as

> a group of musicians who learn, collaborate, create, and make music using any combination of instruments, genres, and styles of music in a learner-centered space. It encourages a diverse combination of instruments, supports innovative music making, and encourages the inclusion of both digital and acoustic instruments.[7]

Since there is no canon of repertoire written specifically for these combinations of instruments, the students must work together to arrange material for the ensemble.

Learning and Assessment

Beginning in the 1970s, schools explored how to use Computer Assisted Instruction (CAI) to help students with keyboard studies, sight-singing, and ear training.[8] Pitch recognition technology has improved significantly over the past few decades, leading to the emergence of apps and software programs that can identify missed notes and rhythms in a student's performance. These include cloud-based programs such as SmartMusic and PracticeFirst. The latter may be used as one component of an online music classroom environment called MusicFirst, which includes DAWs (SoundTrap, Soundation), notation software (Noteflight), music theory (Musition, Auralia), and other creative music-making cloud-based apps. Other cloud-based tools for song-writing help students understand, and hear, the relationships among notes in a given scale. Using the Chrome Music Lab Song Maker or OnlineSequencer. net, students can draw melodies by adding notes to a grid. These tools, and others like them, play the composition back for the student and illustrate a melody using piano roll iconic notation (see Chapter 2 for more information about this notation system).

Visit www.musicfirst.com/software/ to explore a variety of cloud-based apps for music learning and assessment.

Recently, app and software designers have created gamified systems of learning music through iconic notation and tablature, making them appropriate choices for popular music education. These programs (e.g., Yousician, 4Chords, Rocksmith) move learners through sequential content and award points based on rhythmic and tonal accuracy. Yousician (Figure 9.2) is an app

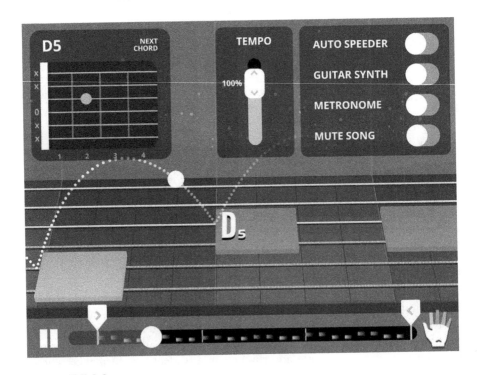

FIGURE 9.2
Yousician App for iOS, Android, MacOS, Windows
Photo retrieved from Yousician.com and reprinted with permission

that teaches guitar, bass, keyboard, voice, and ukulele through point-based leveled challenges using a variety of notations (e.g., five-line staff, tablature, iconic). Many young musicians learn to play instruments in these gamified systems, which are seemingly disconnected from the school music experience. Music teachers may be able to leverage student interest in these apps to help them understand musical concepts and techniques in a popular music classroom environment.

DIFFERENTIATION AND ACCESSIBILITY

Setting Parameters

Many apps and software programs provide customized options that allow teachers to control parameters for individual students. For creative activities, such as improvising and composing, it may be possible to limit the note choices on a keyboard or other virtual instrument in ways not typically possible with live instruments. The keyboard, guitar, bass, and stringed instruments in GarageBand for iOS may be limited to any number of scales (pentatonic, major, minor, blues, etc.), providing less experienced students with fewer options to scaffold their success. Even if this customization is not possible, it will be helpful to some students if there are clear boundaries related to rhythm, melody, and harmony. Just as Picasso discovered new approaches to visual art by limiting himself to variants of blue, students may discover new musical possibilities by limiting the parameters of their work.

Choice

The wide range of choices among apps and software programs offer students multiple access points and vehicles for self-expression. When presented with a choice of applications, and at least a fundamental understanding of how to use them, some students may find that one program or another is best suited to realize their creative goals. A variety of factors may inform these choices, including musical preference, modes of understanding (visual, kinesthetic), and personal taste. One student may find that FL Studio is the best tool to help them create beats for an original rap composition while another student believes Pro Tools is the best tool to produce a new country song. These two students may be working toward the same learning objective, to create an original musical composition, but find they have specific preferences for the tools they use to meet that objective. A facilitator working in a student-centered popular music classroom should be aware of the value of having these choices and allow students the opportunity to explore and work with a variety of apps and software tools.

Students With Physical Disabilities

The act of holding an instrument and physically pressing buttons, keys, or strings, can create obstacles for students with physical disabilities and may prevent them from participating in a musical activity. Apps and software programs offer unique solutions that allow for meaningful participation in

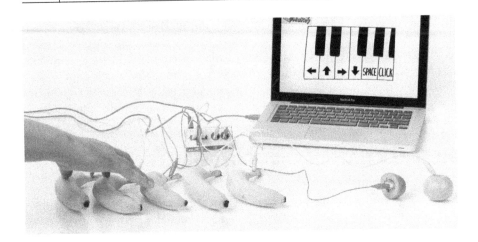

FIGURE 9.3
Makey Makey Hardware and Scratch Studio Computer Software to Perform MIDI Sounds
Retrieved from *http://makeymakey.com* and reproduced with permission

creating and performing music for all students. Many music-making apps (e.g., GarageBand, ThumbJam) are touch-sensitive and do not require a significant amount of physical strength to operate. Some apps require no touch at all, and sound is controlled using a built-in camera (e.g., Airvox) or gyroscope (e.g., Gyro Synth). Scratch is a computer program that works with Makey hardware (Figure 9.3). The program allows students to trigger instrument sounds by touching everyday objects, such as paper, tape, food, and Play-Doh.

CONCLUSION

Apps and software programs have reshaped music education spaces by expanding the possibilities of instruments and performance techniques, allowing for low-cost sound recording and music production activities, and providing customizable learning platforms that engage learners at every ability and level of experience. And while music teachers often struggle to implement creative activities into their music instruction,[9] the programs and technologies outlined in this chapter can engage students in a multitude of creative practices identified by the National Core Arts Standards: imagination, investigation, construction, and reflection in multiple contexts.[10] We recommend that teachers spend some time exploring the apps found in this chapter to determine which programs are particularly well suited for their teaching objectives and the learning goals of their current or future students.

Takeaways

- A variety of apps and software programs enable students to create, perform, record, assess, and share their music.

- Because of the rapid expansion and ever-increasing power of technology, new programs and updates to previous versions are abundant.
- Music teachers should consider the cost, location, ease of use, and most importantly purpose of the technology before determining specific apps and software programs for their class.
- App and software customizations allow for differentiation and increased access for students with special needs.

Discussion Questions

1. What software programs and apps are you most familiar with? What purpose could they meet in a popular music classroom?
2. What are the pros and cons of teaching music technology classes in a shared-use school computer lab?
3. What kind of music apps would you like to see in the future?
4. How do apps and software programs promote inclusion in a popular music classroom?

Notes

1 Waldrop, "Moore's Law," 144.
2 Rideout and Katz, *Technology and Learning in Lower-Income Families.*
3 "National Core Arts Standards."
4 Cremata et al., *The Music Learning Profiles Project.*
5 Williams, "iPad is a REAL Musical Instrument," 93–98.
6 Ibid.
7 Kladder, "Non-Traditional Secondary Music Performance Class."
8 Eddins, "Computer-Assisted Instruction in Music," 7–14.
9 Byo, "Perceived Ability to Implement the National Standards," 111–23.
10 "Conceptual Framework for Arts Learning."

Digital Audio Workstations

The DAW is one of the most versatile musical tools of the 21st century. The term applies to both hardware configurations (e.g., computers with audio interfaces and recording software, standalone devices) and software applications (e.g., GarageBand, Audacity, FruityLoops/FL Studio, Soundtrap, Pro Tools, and Logic), which will all be explored in this chapter. These tools are more readily available and accessible to our students than any musical instrument, other than the voice, and software-based DAWs are sometimes free and run on multiple devices, including smartphones. Many general music teachers have designed classroom projects using DAWs,[1] and there is a tremendous opportunity to engage learners at every grade level, including those in performing ensembles, in collaborative work through sound recording technology. Some DAWs are user-friendly with drag-and-drop features that allow a novice to quickly create an arrangement using prerecorded loops – a very popular, if not overused, DAW-based classroom activity. Students may also use the instruments contained within a DAW to reproduce popular music songs by transcribing and performing the individual parts as separate tracks (e.g., keys, guitar, bass, drum kit). Amateur and professional producers find DAWs to be powerful instruments for creating original content. These tools can be used to create, produce, write, and edit musical ideas individually or in collaboration with others. While technology-based school composing and arranging activities were once limited to notation-based software programs, DAWs offer a relatively new space for creative music-making experiences requiring no prerequisite knowledge of music theory or traditional staff notation.

BASICS

Recording Audio and MIDI

Audio refers to any sound that is recorded with a microphone, acoustic instrument, or electric instrument. Audio is usually transmitted through cables with 1/4 inch or XLR cables and connectors, although some devices use USB connectors (see Chapter 11 for a complete description of cables and

FIGURE 10.1
Audio Sound Wave

connectors). Audio often appears as a sound wave in the display window of a DAW (Figure 10.1).

The speed (tempo) and frequency (pitch) of an audio recording may be manipulated, but this results in a mild to severe change of timbre, depending on the degree of the change and the quality of the software. Audio regions are often designated with a different color from MIDI regions in a DAW to make it easier to identify the classification of various tracks.

MIDI is an acronym for Musical Instrument Digital Interface. It is not a *real* sound in the sense that it requires special equipment to be performed and heard. In other words, there are no acoustic MIDI instruments. There are, however, recorded samples of acoustic instruments that may be triggered and sounded by a MIDI device. MIDI recordings are typically produced by performing on a MIDI keyboard controller (Figure 10.2) or MIDI drum pad controller, which transmits information to another device that contains a bank of MIDI sounds. Most modern MIDI controllers connect to hardware through USB cables or Bluetooth connections. MIDI information is often displayed using piano roll notation in most DAW programs (Figure 10.3). The bars on the piano roll notation correspond to a given pitch triggered by a controller (e.g., C1 triggers a kick drum sound when working with drum tracks) and indicate the duration of the note by length. Unlike audio, the speed (tempo) and frequency (pitch) of a MIDI recording may be manipulated without any loss of sound quality. A MIDI recording originally produced using a keyboard sound may be changed to a trumpet, violin, or any other instrument with the click (or tap) of a button. These features make MIDI a useful tool for

FIGURE 10.2
MIDI Keyboard Controller

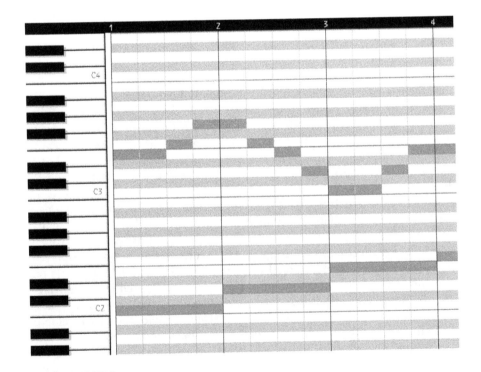

FIGURE 10.3
MIDI Data Displayed in Piano Roll Notation
Kanohara / Wikimedia Commons / CC-BY-SA-3.0

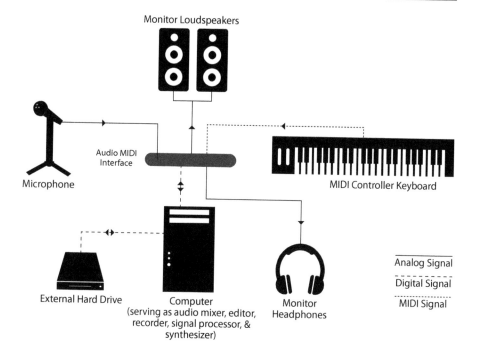

FIGURE 10.4
Signal Flow Diagram

composition and arranging with instruments that may not be readily accessible or easily performed.

An **audio interface** translates a sound recorded by a microphone or electric instrument into digital information that may be processed by a computer, mobile device, or digital multitrack recorder. Once the information is processed by these devices, an audio interface will translate the signal back into audible form to be heard through **monitors** (speakers) or headphones. Because DAWs often involve a combination of MIDI and audio sounds, it is important to understand how these signals move between pieces of equipment; this is known as **signal flow** (Figure 10.4).

MULTITRACK RECORDING

Multitrack recording is at the very heart of the DAW. This term describes the ability to simultaneously record multiple channels, or tracks, of discrete sounds. The process began in the 1950s using analog tape but has since evolved to include digital (computer-based) platforms widely accessible to consumers, reaching a professional-level quality in the 2000s.

CHOOSING A DAW

The choice of a DAW configuration depends on several factors: experience level, classroom space, allotted time, budget, and personal preference. There are appropriate choices for every grade level and teaching situation, from an elementary school general music classroom to a high school music production lab. We will explore some of the most common DAW setups: multitrack recorders, DAW apps on tablets, and DAW software on computers, and consider the pros and cons of each in a variety of contexts.

Standalone Digital Multitrack Recorders

Standalone digital multitrack recorders include a hard disk for recording and saving files, a mixing console, audio and MIDI inputs, a screen to view the project, and outputs for headphones and monitors, all in one device. These types of DAW do not require a computer or software program and may be ideal for classrooms that do not have access to computers and tablets, or for teachers who do not have a primary classroom space (i.e., classrooms on a cart). Because digital multitrack recorders are standalone units, there are no problems related to incompatible devices, system upgrades, software freezes/crashes, and other unpredictable issues that arise when using computer-based DAWs. When working with a digital multitrack recorder, students plug instruments and microphones into the device, set recording levels, and record directly to the unit, generally using headphones for **monitoring** (hearing what you play as you record) and playback. Digital multitrack recorders have mixing and editing capabilities and will export audio files to a flash drive. These devices may not easily be updated or upgraded, meaning that one unit will typically have the same features and functions year after year, despite rapid advances in technology (see Moore's Law from Chapter 9: Apps and Software). These devices declined in popularity as software-based DAWs became more prevalent, but they are still widely used today. Multitrack recorders come in a variety of sizes, and average costs range from $100 to $1,000. A multitrack recorder with eight inputs, meaning it can record eight instruments or voices at once, is pictured in Figure 10.5. Keep in mind that The Beatles recorded many legendary hits on a four-track recorder; more is not necessarily better!

Mobile-Based DAWs

The most popular DAW configuration for both classroom and personal use is a smartphone, iPad, tablet, or Chromebook with a sound recording/editing app, such as GarageBand. According to a 2017 report from the Pew Research Center, 96 percent of young adults in the United States live in a household with at least one smartphone.[2] This means that most students have access to a (potential) DAW in their very own homes. The quality of recordings produced by a free mobile-based DAW may be indistinguishable from the level of recordings produced in multimillion dollar recording studios just decades ago. Famous hip hop artists, including Kanye West and Kendrick Lamar, have used GarageBand on their iPhone to record songs for their albums, and students in

FIGURE 10.5
Digital Multitrack Recorder
Jud McCranie at English Wikipedia / CC-BY-SA-3.0

classrooms across the United States are producing and sharing professional-sounding original music using mobile-based DAWs. While microphones, headphones, and audio interfaces are not required to use a mobile DAW, they may help to improve the quality of the recorded sound and provide a means by which to monitor (hear) a song as it is being recorded or edited. Mobile-based DAWs offer multitrack recording (up to 32 tracks in the current GarageBand 2.3.8 for iOS) and several features not often found on standalone or computer-based DAWs: touch-based virtual instruments, touch-based looping tools, video lessons, and Bluetooth sharing. Best of all, most mobile-based DAWs are intuitive and fairly easy to use. If your district has access to Chromebooks or other cloud-based technology, Soundtrap and Soundation Studio are excellent DAW options.

Mobile-based technology is widespread in schools, as these tools have many other applications beyond music production and can easily be stored on a cart and shared among faculty. For these reasons, mobile-based DAWs are probably the most logical and cost-efficient option for music classrooms engaging in beginning- to intermediate-level music production activities. Mobile devices typically cost between $500 and $1,000 (and may be shared across the district), and DAW apps are typically inexpensive or free; GarageBand 2.1 for iOS became free to users in 2017, for example. Mobile-compatible microphones cost between $50 and $200.

Computer-Based DAWs

While standalone recorders and mobile-based apps offer portable and cost-efficient options for sound recording technology, they are not industry-standard tools and may not be the most appropriate choice for an advanced music production class. Computer-based DAWs (see Figure 10.6) provide the maximum amount of processing power and increased number of options and tools for: advanced editing techniques, working with video, using MIDI controllers, and expansions of sound recording equipment (headphone amplifiers, audio effects processors, mixing desks, electronic drums, Ableton devices, samplers, etc.) that more accurately resemble technologies used in the music industry. While a dedicated music technology lab would be most preferable, any school computer lab can function as a space for DAWs at no additional cost. Examples of free DAW computer-based software include:

FIGURE 10.6
Digital Audio Workstation
Photo courtesy of Steve Holley

Audacity (a DAW with somewhat limited capabilities for Windows and MacOS) and GarageBand (a more versatile DAW, for MacOS). Cloud-based options, which work on all platforms with an internet browser, include Soundation Studio, BandLab, Soundtrap, and AudioTool. Cloud-based options are usually free or require a low monthly subscription. Of course, more expensive DAW options exist, and are frequently used in the music industry. Logic (for MacOS) and Pro Tools (for Windows and MacOS) are significantly more expensive, with higher monthly subscription fees or a hefty one-time license purchase, but provide more options for recording, editing, mixing, and mastering. These tools also have the most significant learning curve and are far from intuitive. However, experienced users of GarageBand may find that a natural step up is Logic, which has a similar look and feel to the desktop version of GarageBand.

Unlike standalone devices, and to some extent mobile-based devices, computer-based DAWs are easily customizable. One of the most important hardware components of the computer-based DAW is the audio interface. An audio interface is a piece of hardware that allows the user to plug in microphones and electronic instruments to connect to the computer while serving as a preamp to boost the signal from the microphone or instrument. You can buy a good quality audio interface for between $100 and $200. The built-in microphone on a computer could suffice as an audio interface, but most entry-level music tech labs include a quality USB microphone at the very least. These USB microphones typically start at $100 and many provide headphone outputs for zero-latency monitoring. This means there is no delay between when a sound is performed and when it is heard in the headphones. **Latency** may be defined as the time it takes to process the original sound signal and send it to the headphones or monitors.

APPROACHES

The DAW is a multifaceted tool that has applications for performance, production, and recording. We will examine each of these functions in the following section and consider how each might be realized in a variety of K-12 classroom situations.

Instruments for Live Performance

The **virtual instruments** included in many DAW apps may be performed live in tablet or iPad ensembles. The University of Southern Florida developed an ensemble called "Touch" which set a precedent for using exclusively technology-based instruments in a school performing ensemble.

Visit http://popmusicped.com for a TEDx video link featuring the ensemble facilitator, David Williams, explaining the function of a DAW as an ensemble instrument.

Virtual instruments could be used to replicate typical popular music instrumentation (keys, guitars, bass, and drums) or instruments that are unique to the device. In Chapter 12: Making the Band, we will examine an application of DAWs in both digital ensembles and hybrid ensembles, which combine acoustic and digital instruments together in one space.

Music Production

Music production is the art of making music through any combination of recording tracks, making beats, using samples, and arranging loops. The process may include one person or a team of artists, producers, and audio engineers working together in collaboration. You may wish to divide a class into these responsibilities or have each student serve in all the roles. Either way, individual artists or teams of production groups move through the following sequence of preproduction, production, and postproduction activities.

Preproduction

This is the initial development stage for a musical project. Students should brainstorm or select topic ideas, write lyrics, draft musical arrangements on instruments or a DAW, and reach out to potential collaborators, in or outside of the class, for their project.

Production

Students record the individual tracks for their project – known as **tracking** – during the production phase. This may include recording live instruments, recording MIDI instrument tracks using controllers, or working to arrange prerecorded loops into a larger piece. Instruments may be recorded simultaneously or one at a time. Recording individual instruments at separate times allow for less **bleed** (when the sound of one instrument appears in the track of another) but eliminates the opportunity for live interaction among musicians.

Postproduction

This is the most arduous phase of the production process. Students listen to their recordings repeatedly and make edits to improve the quality of their work. There is a great deal of refinement in commercially produced recordings and an expectation of perfection. Every pitch needs to be accurate and perfectly in tune. Every rhythm should align with the meter of the song unless that is not the intention of the producer. A **quantization** tool is used to adjust all MIDI sounds to a perfect subdivision of note durations, as determined by the engineer. Student producers listen to ensure that each instrument and voice is properly placed in the **mix** (overall balance of the song). Students should consider the **panning** of sounds. This means that some instruments or sounds will be more prominent on one side than the other. Students can visualize the horizontal plane of the recording, meaning which instruments are placed in the far left, near left, center, near right, or far right areas of the mix (imagine or sketch a live group playing on a stage to help with this process). The final stage of postproduction is called **mastering,** a process by which students ensure the dynamic level and equalization of each song is balanced and consistent before making copies or distributing the work.

Once the production process is over, you may wish to share your students' music through a free or paid online streaming platform. This activity could serve as a fundraiser for the school music program. SoundCloud and Bandcamp are two websites that allow musicians to upload their music and receive comments from other users about their music. As long as 100 percent of the music is original, there should be no copyright concerns.

MUSIC PRODUCTION TIP

Here is a quick tip to determine if a mix is balanced. Listen to a section of the song and gradually decrease the volume on the headphones or monitors. Make a note of any voice or instrument that remains after others have disappeared. Students should **attenuate** (decrease) the volume of the loudest tracks to ensure all parts disappear at the same time.

Recording and Assessing Live Performances

Music educators have recognized the value of recording live performances as an assessment practice for nearly a century. In a 1936 issue of *Music Educators Journal*, Charles Kettering wrote that "recording is the greatest aid to teaching the twentieth century has yet produced. It provides at once a definite objective in applied music study, and the means for determining when that objective has been reached."[3] While the idea of using live recordings as an assessment tool for school performing ensembles may be obvious, the cross-curricular opportunities to engage music technology students in the process of recording, editing, and documenting these performances may be less apparent. Schools may consider creating a micro-level student-run record label that records, produces, and archives recordings of school concerts. Any of the DAWs described in this chapter would be suitable tools for recording a live concert.

CLASSROOM DESIGN

DAWs may be utilized in virtually any classroom space on any budget. One author of this book, Matthew Clauhs, taught music production classes in a room that was void of computers, tablets, or any other form of technology. In this classroom, students simply brought whatever technology they had from home or borrowed a device from the school. There was no clean-up, no wires, no broken equipment, and students could easily complete homework assignments on the very same technology they used in the classroom. A step

FIGURE 10.7
A Single-DAW Recording Studio
Photo courtesy of Joel Smales

up from this design might include a mobile technology cart or a school computer lab that is not a dedicated music space. If there is a budget to purchase music-specific technology and equipment, the following classroom setups are worth exploring.

The Single-DAW Recording Studio

If you are interested in having students work in collaborative teams to produce a single product, a recording studio may be an appropriate classroom design (Figure 10.7). This setup would include a single DAW and plenty of space for tracking instruments. The recording studio might feature an isolation booth for recording vocals in a well-designed acoustic space, and **gobos** (movable walls) that create separation between instruments, minimizing bleed. The DAW in the studio would likely include a computer with professional sound recording software (e.g., Pro Tools, Logic), an audio interface that could handle a larger number of inputs (between 8 and 32), and components that complement and extend the possibilities of the workstation, including a mixing desk, a variety of MIDI controllers, effects processors, headphone amplifiers, and high-quality monitors. Since a recording captures the acoustics of the performing space, acoustic treatments should be placed on walls and ceilings, preferably with the consultation of an expert sound engineer. An inspector should also verify that the treatments do not violate any fire code or other school safety regulations.

The Multiple-DAW Technology Lab

If your goal is to have students work independently to create their own individual songs, then a technology lab that contains DAWs for each student would be the most appropriate classroom design. In this setup, students would have their own independent workspace with a slimmed-down version of the equipment described in the recording studio. Headphones would replace studio monitors since it is not practical to have multiple stations playing simultaneously out loud. A basic DAW setup might include a computer running sound recording software, an audio interface with one or two inputs for a microphone and/or instrument, a small MIDI keyboard controller, and a pair of headphones. Ideally, there would be a way to broadcast individual student workstations to a larger screen and setup of studio monitors, so that students could share their individual work with the class for feedback.

FUNDRAISING OPPORTUNITIES

There are several fundraising opportunities and grants available for school programs wishing to integrate technology into the curriculum, particularly in high-poverty school districts. Visit http://popmusicped.com for updated links with resources to fund technology. Examples are:

- Donorschoose.org
- Adopt-a-classroom
- We are Teachers
- The Mockingbird Foundation
- Career and Technical Education (CTE) grants.

DIFFERENTIATION

DAWs allow students of varying abilities and experience levels to produce professional-sounding music. Advanced students should be encouraged to write original music by sequencing MIDI with controllers and recording audio using real instruments. Intermediate-level students could produce a combination of original audio and prerecorded loops (e.g., record a single vocal track over a background of loops). Beginning-level students could create a new work simply by dragging and dropping prerecorded loops into a template. Regardless of their ability or experience level, all students should engage in some individual and collaborative work to contribute to the larger whole. Students could align their individual projects to focus on a single topic, perhaps generating a class album unified by a common theme.

Sound recording technology may appeal to students who have less experience or interest in existing school music ensembles, creating more opportunities to participate in school music. New York music teacher, Brian Franco, created a course titled *Music Industry* that allowed students to choose from several roles in music production: songwriters, performing artists, producers, audio engineers, and video engineers. Students researched those roles and worked collaboratively in a project-based environment, toward a common goal of releasing an album or music video. Mr. Franco lobbied to the New York board of regents who eventually voted to allow *Music Industry* to serve as an alternative to the secondary general music class titled *Music in our Lives*. Mr. Franco witnessed dramatic increases within the school music department as more students saw themselves as music-makers in the curriculum.

DAW technologies may allow students with limited physical mobility to participate in an ensemble or recording project. Chapter 9: Apps and Software explored a variety of apps that allow students to make music by moving their bodies in ways that engage learners varying abilities like never before. Students could also play virtual instruments on a DAW App such as GarageBand, which requires far less strength or dexterity than performing the same part on an acoustic instrument.

CONCLUSION

DAWs provide new opportunities to engage learners in creative practices identified by the National Core Arts Standards: imagination, investigation, construction, and reflection in multiple contexts. Music educators may find that DAW spaces are ideal for learner-led experiences that are facilitated, not directed, by a teacher-producer who collaborates with artists to help them reach their full potential. These technologies and approaches could help music educators to transform classrooms into studio spaces that leverage the creativity and musical interests of the learners in the school.

Takeaways

- There are DAW options (standalone multitrack recorders, mobile-based apps, computer-based software) and customizable hardware configurations that cater to the unique needs of individual learners in any classroom context.
- DAWs are versatile devices that may be used as instruments within a performance or tools for music production and sound recording.
- Music production projects allow for a great deal of differentiation, as students can choose production roles that suit their preferences and abilities or work on the same project through multiple entry points.

Discussion Questions

1. Which DAW classroom configuration would work best for your current/future music teaching situation? Consider the hardware, software,

and classroom design choices presented in this chapter to explain your decisions.

2.   What are the benefits or limitations of having a school iPad band, or a similar DAW performing ensemble?
3.   What are some ways that a music production class using DAWs could complement a traditional school music program?

Notes

1   Clauhs, Franco, and Cremata, "Music Production in School Music Programs," 55–63.
2   Rainie and Perrin, "10 Fact About Smartphones."
3   Kettering, "Recording Procedure in Music Education," 29–84.

Live Sound and Recording

If you have ever looked at pieces of audio equipment and wondered (1) what all the buttons, faders, and knobs control; (2) how one unit connects to another; and (3) which cable to use and where to plug it in, you are not alone! Many teacher preparation programs do not provide pre-service teachers with adequate knowledge and skills required to operate live sound and recording equipment despite the necessity of these skills when on the job. While the same pieces of sound equipment may vary by brand and model, a fundamental understanding of how this gear works will help an individual navigate most studio desks, sound modules, and mixing boards with familiarity and ease. In this chapter, live sound generally refers to the miking, mixing, and amplification of live performances in front of an audience while recording refers to the miking, recording, mixing, and mastering of studio or live sessions. There is overlap in these two areas and we will highlight how these contexts relate to specific pieces of equipment and different techniques throughout the chapter.

MICROPHONES

Microphones convert sound into electrical signals that are amplified or recorded. This conversion may be accomplished through a variety of ways, and each process corresponds to a different type of microphone (e.g., dynamic, condenser, ribbon, carbon, fiber optic). An understanding of these technical processes is not essential to popular music education and beyond the scope of this book; however, knowing which microphone is appropriate to use in a given context is essential, and that information will be the focus of this section.

Types
The most common type of microphone found in school settings is a **dynamic microphone**, which is relatively inexpensive and more durable when compared to others. The Shure SM57 (typically used for instruments) and SM58 (typically used for vocals) are industry-standard dynamic microphones found

everywhere from school concert halls to professional performance venues. These microphones are well worth the investment and may be used to accomplish nearly every objective in live sound and recording studio settings, including miking live vocals, live instruments, drums, and electric guitar amplifiers. Dynamic microphones can handle loud sound sources with ease, making them particularly well suited for louder instruments and live performances, such as popular music concerts.

Although dynamic microphones may be used to record instruments and voices in a studio setting as well, a quality **condenser microphone** would produce a better recording. Condenser microphones tend to be more expensive than dynamic microphones, although it is possible to find decent microphones at a lower price range, including those in the popular MXL brand of microphones. These microphones are much more sensitive than dynamic microphones, which makes them ideal for studio settings, but not always appropriate for noisy live sound environments. It is often more difficult to get separation between instruments when using condenser microphones as compared to dynamic microphones, resulting in bleed from one sound source into a microphone being used to capture something else. Audio engineers place movable walls between sound sources to minimize this bleed in a studio setting, but this is not always practical in a live performance, hence the use of dynamic microphones for live sound. Condenser microphones also require a 48-volt charge called **phantom power** to work. When plugging a condenser microphone into a mixing board or console, look for a button that has a +48v sign. Plug the microphone into the device and then push the phantom power button to provide a charge that will power the microphone. Avoid pushing the button before plugging the microphone in or using phantom power with any microphone that does not require it.

Patterns

The location and amount of sound that dynamic and condenser microphones capture will vary based on the pattern of the microphone. These patterns include: **cardioid, super cardioid, omnidirectional, and bidirectional** (see Figure 11.1).

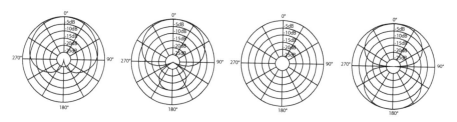

FIGURE 11.1
Cardioid, Super Cardioid, Omnidirectional, and Bidirectional (from left to right)

Cardioid

Also known as unidirectional, these microphones record sounds located in a heart-shaped pattern from the microphone (hence the cardio root in its name). This is the pattern used in the classic Shure SM57/58 microphones. Simply put, these microphones mostly capture what is directly in front of them, within a foot or so. Dynamic and condenser microphones with a cardioid pattern have many applications and should be a staple of the school's microphone inventory.

Super Cardioid

Also known as hypercardioid or hyperdirectional microphones, these also record sounds directly in front of the microphone, but with greater depth and not as much width. If your sound source is more than a few feet away from the microphone, you might wish to use a super cardioid pattern, as these microphones are less likely to cause **feedback**, noise that results from a sound source looping itself through a microphone and nearby speaker, when compared to other types. Musical productions and film crews use super cardioid microphones to pick up actors from more than a few feet away without capturing the whole stage or getting in the way of the scene.

Omnidirectional

Not surprisingly, these microphones capture a sound source from every direction and may be a suitable choice to record a group of musicians arranged in a circle around the microphone. Audio engineers may also use omnidirectional microphones to add room noise to a mix, resulting in a more natural-sounding acoustical environment. Lavalier mikes are often omnidirectional.

Bidirectional

Also known as *figure 8*, these microphone patterns capture sound equally from either side of the microphone. They are a strong choice for recording two musicians standing on either side of the microphone.

Some microphones have switches that allow the user to change the setting of the microphone between cardioid, omnidirectional, and bidirectional patterns, such as the Blue Yeti USB microphone in Figure 11.2. All of these microphones may be connected via audio connectors (1/4 inch, XLR) or by a digital USB connector. We will explain more about specific types of microphone cables, such as XLR, later in this chapter. USB microphones are becoming increasingly popular because they do not require an additional audio interface. USB microphones often include an onboard preamp and an analog-to-digital (A/D) converter. The preamp eliminates the need to be connected to a mixer or external mic preamp. The A/D converter makes USB mics ideal for mobile digital recording with DAW software or other recording software.

Microphone Placement

Once you have established which microphone is most appropriate for the classroom, studio, or performance space, you will need to know where to place it for the best possible sound. A variety of factors will influence the

FIGURE 11.2
Four Pattern Choices in One USB Microphone

distance that the microphone should be placed from the sound source. **Close miking** (also called spot miking) is a technique that places the microphone no more than two feet from the sound source, while **distant miking** is a technique that places the microphone more than two feet from the sound source. Using a dynamic cardioid microphone (e.g., Shure SM57/58) with a close miking technique will minimize bleed in a live performance, but may fail to capture the natural sound of the instrument or voice as heard from a few feet away in a studio setting. Some engineers will use two microphones, one close to and one distant from the sound source, to create a more complete sonic image of the instrument or voice. Distant miking would also be an appropriate choice when working with a large ensemble, as it creates a balanced sound and avoids picking up individual players in the group.

Live sound engineers may sometimes place a microphone near (or sometimes in) the bell or sound hole of an acoustic instrument. While this placement does not capture the nuances of the instrument, it can help to minimize bleed if another sound source, such as a crash cymbal, is near the instrument's microphone. Whenever possible, use a condenser cardioid microphone to record acoustic instruments and guitar/bass amplifiers in a studio setting to capture the full frequency range (from the lowest note to highest overtone) of the instrument. Use the following microphone placement guidelines in recording situations and in a well-isolated performance space.

- *Acoustic instruments.* Brass instruments should be miked slightly off-center from the bell (typically with a dynamic mic); flute microphones should be placed near the nose of the player; other woodwinds sound best when miked near the middle of the instrument (as opposed to the bell); and stringed instruments and acoustic guitars should be recorded

6–12 inches away, with the microphone directed toward the area where the bow, finger, or pic meets the strings (e.g., near the bridge). More sensitive microphones (e.g., condenser and ribbon) should not be placed too closely to a loud sound source.

- *Amplifiers.* Place the microphone an inch or two away from the amplifier, pointed at the cone of the speaker.
- *Drum kit.* Drum kits are the most challenging instrument to mike, because there are many individual instruments with a variety of frequencies all grouped together in a small space. For large auditoriums or outdoor gigs, miking the bass drum will help to provide a fuller sound since the high frequency pitches of the cymbals and snare drum travel much farther than the lower frequencies of the bass drum. Some manufacturers sell packages that include microphones designed for each specific instrument (bass drum, snare, toms, cymbals, hi-hats, etc.). Keep in mind that miking this many instruments will require a lot of channels on your mixing and/or recording devices, cables, training, and patience.
- *Vocals.* When performing live, vocalists should hold a dynamic cardioid microphone no more than two inches from the mouth. A simple way to measure this distance is by placing two fingers between your mouth and the microphone. Vocalists can also create different effects by cupping their hands around the microphone or singing right next to the microphone, which will produce a **proximity effect**, giving the vocals more low end. When recording vocalists, condenser cardioid microphones should be placed in front of the vocalist's mouth, or slightly off-center to alleviate plosives, which are "tuh" "kuh" and "puh" sounds, that distort the recording. A pop shield (Figure 11.3) or wind guard may further alleviate plosives from the recording.

Stereo Microphone Techniques

Two microphones may be used to capture a natural stereo field of a sound source. This technique is known as **stereo miking,** and it allows the listener to hear different instruments and voices in each ear. This is particularly useful when miking a grand piano or drum kit, as these instruments sound differently in the left and right ears of the performer, or a live performance that is experienced in stereo by an audience member.

The XY technique replicates the sonic image that a pair of ears would perceive listening in the audience. It is important to use two cardioid (directional) microphones when using this technique. The spaced stereo technique captures the left and right side of a stage. When using this technique be sure that the distance between the microphones is at least three times greater than the distance from the microphone to the source of the sound (Figure 11.4). This is known as the **3:1 rule.** If you are recording a choir that is five feet away, then the second microphone should be roughly fifteen feet away from the first.

There are infinite ways to set up microphones in live performance and studio settings, but the above guidelines should work well in most contexts.

FIGURE 11.3
Pop Shield with a Condenser Microphone in a Studio Setting
Photo by Leo Wieling on Unsplash.com

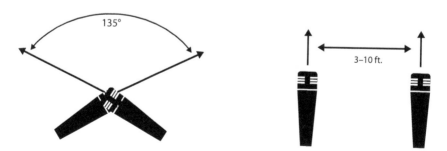

FIGURE 11.4
XY and Spaced Pair Stereo Microphone Techniques

These are common, time-tested approaches and have worked well for many music teachers and audio engineers. Experiment with a variety of microphones and placement techniques to find the sound that works best for you and your students. Be sure to involve them in the process, as learning about microphone technique is a major component of popular music education. Students will want this knowledge and skill set so they can run sound and recording sessions of their own.

CABLES AND CONNECTORS

XLR cables are often used to connect microphones to mixers or other interfaces, but they are also sometimes used to connect amplifiers, mixers, and speakers. Most XLR cables will have male-to-female connections, meaning that one side has three pins (male) and the other side does not (female). Five-pin XLR cables exist but are not as common as the three-pin connector. The signal of an XLR cable moves in the direction of the pins, meaning that the male side will connect to the mixer, audio interface, or any other piece of gear that is receiving the signal, while the female side connects to a microphone or any piece of gear that is sending a signal.

Stereo/TRS (tip-ring-sleeve) cables look very similar to mono/TS (tip-sleeve) cables but have one important difference, an additional plastic divider that creates a separate ring on the TRS connector (see Figure 11.5). The additional ring on the TRS connector allows for a stereo signal, which carries two separate lines that may be assigned to two separate tracks or the left and right channel of a single stereo track. This is very useful when connecting instruments or gear that is performed in stereo, such as keyboards which may pan the sides of the instrument to the left and right channels of the mix. Headphones use TRS connectors for this very reason, to create a more natural sonic image as our ears pick up different sounds from the left and right side of a room in everyday life.

A mono/TS (tip-sleeve) cable is used to connect an electric instrument (e.g., guitar, bass, sequencer, synthesizer) to a mixer or other interface. These types of cables are called instrument cables and they contain two male connectors, which may be plugged in either direction. A different type of mono/TS cable is a patch cable, which is usually shorter in length and designed to connect two pieces of audio gear together. A third type of mono/TS cable is a speaker cable, which is usually thicker and contains different wiring from an instrument cable. Be sure to look at the label of the cable to determine if it should be used with speakers or instruments, as they are not interchangeable. For

FIGURE 11.5
XLR Cable, Stereo/TRS Cable, Mono/TS Cable, A/B USB Cable (from left to right)

example, if you use a speaker cable with a guitar, you may hear a buzzing sound or even a radio station coming out of the amplifier. And if you use an instrument cable to connect speakers to a PA system, the shielding around the wires can actually melt due to the high amount of current going through the cable!

USB cables are more commonly used to connect pieces of digital audio gear and MIDI devices. Microphones that have a built-in audio interface (see Chapter 10 for more information about audio interfaces) will connect to a computer using a USB cable. USB cables are not often used in live sound contexts by audio engineers unless they are using a digital connection on a mixing board to connect to a computer for recording or digital processing effects. The A connector of a USB cable is flat and rectangular, while the B connector of a USB cable is shaped more like a square. Typically, the B connector will attach to the audio gear while the A connector links to the computer or laptop. A USB-C connector was released in 2014, and some pieces of audio gear may now include this connection type. The C connector is small and rectangular, allowing for connections to smaller devices.

MIXERS

There is nothing cooler, and perhaps more intimidating than a mixing board in all its glory – with flashing lights and meters, colorful buttons, automated-faders, and endless rows of knobs and dials. This piece of equipment is incredibly versatile, and the many varieties of analog and digital mixers may seem overwhelming at first. Fortunately, all mixers have some universal commonalities, and a fundamental understanding of how a basic channel strip works will help you navigate almost any mixing device.

The Channel Strip

Once you understand how one **channel strip** (Figure 11.6) works on a mixer, then you will understand them all. Fortunately, mixers generally contain the same essential functions (e.g., gain, panning, EQ, etc.) whether they are hardware- or software-based, digital or analog, and used for recording purposes or for live sound. The biggest difference you will find between software and hardware mixers is how you control them, with a mouse or with your hand. Hardware mixers will also have inputs and outputs for you to plug in instruments and playback devices, while software mixers run on a computer that is connected to another interface with these hardware inputs and outputs. You will need enough inputs to accommodate the maximum number of voices and instruments that you want to amplify or record.

The top of the channel strip usually contains a **trim knob** that adjusts the volume, also known as gain, of the signal. If you are using a microphone, you will likely need to turn the trim knob to the right to amplify the signal. Do so until a light indicates that the peak of the signal is close to the top of the meter, without clipping. A warning sign for clipping usually appears as a red light, or

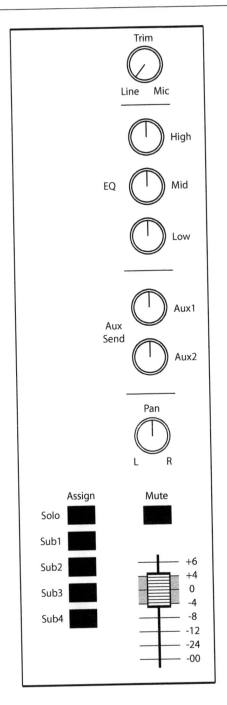

FIGURE 11.6
The Basic Channel Strip

the level meter will turn red. If the input is coming from a piece of gear with a line-level output (e.g., the line out of a guitar/bass amplifier), then the signal is already very strong and the trim knob should be rotated toward the left. If you are using a condenser microphone with phantom power, the +48v sign may appear near the trim knob as well.

The middle of the channel strip usually contains knobs for **EQ** (short for equalization) and **Aux sends**. Digital mixers may have buttons to add EQ and processing effects here as well. EQ controls the amount of low, middle, and high frequencies for each of the channels. You can explore adjustments to these knobs to sculpt the sound that you want. If you or your students aren't sure which adjustments sound best, you can leave these flat, which means right in the middle (pointed up toward 12 o'clock). The aux sends (or effects plugins on a digital mixer) allow the signal to be processed with reverb, delay, chorus, and other options for effects. The send knobs control how much of the signal is processed. Aux/sends may be a more advanced technique of mixing, and fortunately many DAWs have great sounding presets for delay, reverb, and other effects that make this process much easier for the teacher or student sound engineer.

The bottom of the channel strip may include a pan knob, which controls how much of the signal is sent to the left and right sides of the mix. Below the mute button in Figure 11.6 is a **fader**, a sliding rectangular-shaped tool that controls the level (i.e., volume) of the channel going out to the recording device or amplifier. We know this seems like a lot and can be confusing. Check out http://popmusicped.com for videos about navigating a mixer.

QUICK GUIDE TO SETTING LEVELS ON A MIXER

- Plug in microphones and instruments while the channel is muted, or the mixer is powered off.
- Turn the mixer on, but keep channels muted.
- Turn on phantom power (+48v), only if using condenser microphones.
- Set all channel faders to unity gain (0db).
- Make sure all EQ levels are flat.
- One at a time, unmute each channel and adjust the trim knob of each channel until the level sounds right for the room without clipping.
- If it is difficult to hear an instrument or voice, make room for it in the mix by lowering the faders of the other channels.

AMPLIFICATION AND RECORDING

The **main outputs** of the mixing device may be routed to a PA (public address) system in live sound situations. Most digital mixers used as part of a DAW (see Chapter 10) connect to a computer or laptop using a USB cable, so the

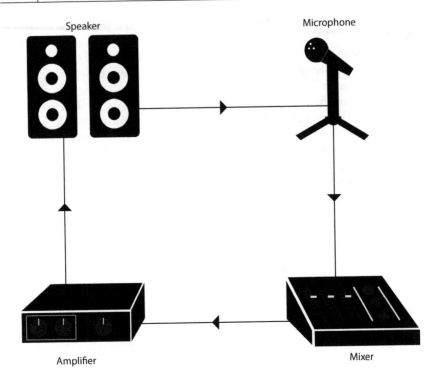

FIGURE 11.7
Mixer Connected to an Amplifier and Passive Speakers

sound is not directly routed, but rather converted to a digital format that can be processed and recorded by a software program. Many live sound systems and recording studios have **passive speakers,** which means the signal coming from the mixer must be routed through an amplifier before it may be heard (Figure 11.7).

Powered speakers (also known as active speakers), on the other hand, have a built-in amplifier and may be connected directly to the output of the mixer. Powered speakers may offer more versatility, as they may be used as monitors (for hearing an on-stage mix) and main speakers, without the need for additional equipment. The drawback is that they tend to be much heavier and more expensive than passive speakers. Some manufacturers produce all-in-one portable systems that include a mixer/amplifier combo along with a pair of lightweight passive speakers. The entire system may be carried in one hand and is affordable for many school budgets. The Fender Passport system and the JBL EON208P are two examples of all-in-one systems. Some of these systems also have Bluetooth capability, allowing wireless connections to smartphones, tablets, computers, and other devices (Figure 11.8).

While an all-in-one system might not provide enough power for a very large venue, it is perfect for smaller performance spaces. It is portable, convenient,

FIGURE 11.8
All-In-One PA System

affordable, and easy to use. The simplicity of these systems makes them a great choice for teachers and students with less sound engineering experience.

DIRECT BOX

Also known as a DI box, a **direct box** (Figure 11.9) converts instrument signals (often with a 1/4 connection) to be compatible with the microphone input (often with an XLR connection) on a mixing console. This is a useful tool when connecting electric guitars, basses, keyboards, or any instrument with a 1/4-inch instrument level output to a mixer with an XLR cable.

DESIGNING LIVE SOUND AND RECORDING SPACES

In addition to the creative music production approaches outlined in Chapter 10: Digital Audio Workstations, live sound and recording principles may be specifically applied to technology classes and broadly integrated into all popular music classes and performances. Some music teachers have created microcosms of the music industry in their school music programs, empowering students to operate live sound and recording equipment to capture performances or produce original albums of their own.[1] This process allows for more student ownership of their work, which typically aids in the development of intrinsic motivation for learning. The following section outlines a variety of ways to utilize live sound and recording technology in classroom and performance spaces. The specific equipment used in these diagrams may vary based on the

FIGURE 11.9
DIRECT BOX
Bene / Wikimedia Commons / CC-BY-SA-3.0

size of the space and the budget of the school, but these guidelines may be a helpful starting place.

Technology Lab

Any school computer classroom or cart with laptop/mobile technology may serve as a music technology lab. Even an empty classroom could work, with students bringing their own devices into and out of the space.

Basic Features

If you can complement an existing computer lab, or have a dedicated music technology classroom, here are some basic features to consider:

- mobile or computer-based DAW;
- MIDI keyboard controller;
- headphones; and
- USB microphone or 2-channel audio interface with XLR and 1/4 inch inputs.

Ideally, each student station would have a complete DAW, which could be anything from a Chromebook running Soundtrap to a full computer station with an audio interface running GarageBand, Logic, Pro Tools, or any other DAW software package. If the station is computer-based, then a MIDI keyboard controller would allow students to create MIDI tracks, compose, program drum grooves, and practice the keyboard. Headphones minimize noise and audio tracks may be recorded with the aid of a USB microphone or a 2-channel audio interface. The audio interface would allow students to directly record instruments, such as electric guitar, electric bass, keyboard, or an electronic drum set, without the use of a microphone. This technique eliminates unwanted room noise and allows for a complete separation of tracks.

Silent Rehearsal Space

Rock band rehearsals have never been quieter thanks to the development of silent rehearsal devices. These digital mixers allow multiple individuals to plug in instruments and microphones that may be monitored through headphones. Classrooms may contain multiple silent rehearsal stations allowing several ensembles to rehearse and record simultaneously without disturbing one another.

Basic Features

The basic features required include:

- digital multitrack recorder/mixer (such as Roland HS-5);
- EDK, electric guitar, electric bass, keyboards;
- dynamic microphones, stands, cables, and headphones.

Ideally, silent rehearsal spaces would use electronic instruments and gear that plug directly into the mixer without the need for amplifiers or microphones. Acoustic instruments and voices may be included, but this will create some noise that may interfere with nearby silent rehearsal stations. Many digital multitrack recorders/mixers that are specifically designed for silent rehearsals, such as the Roland HS-5, allow users to record a digital audio file directly to a USB drive or other device. These devices do not often include phantom power, so dynamic microphones would be preferable in this situation. Dynamic cardioid microphones will also be less likely to pick up other stations.

Live Performance Venue

Many schools with auditoriums have a built-in sound system, but it may be worthwhile to purchase a transportable PA system for performances in other venues.

Basic Features

A basic PA system will include the following features:

- two main speakers;
- two stage monitors;
- amplifier (if speakers and monitors are not powered);
- 4–16 channel mixing board;
- selection of microphones;
- a few dozen XLR cables, patch cables, and microphone stands.

This equipment is often available in a package deal from many manufacturers and music retailers. If there is a limited budget or space for this kind of equipment, consider the all-in-one PA systems described in the previous section.

Recording Studio

A recording studio will offer students an opportunity to produce higher quality recordings than they would create in music technology classrooms or on a silent rehearsal mixer, and with larger groups of musicians. Ideally, a recording studio would include both a **control room**, where the audio engineer and producer would be located, and a **tracking room**, where the artists would perform using their voices and instruments.

Basic Features

A basic recording studio setup would include the following features.

- computer-based DAW (see Chapter 10);
- studio monitors;
- 4–16 channel audio interface with phantom power;
- headphone amplifier;
- selection of microphones;
- a few dozen XLR cables, patch cables, microphone stands, and headphones;
- acoustic treatments (optional).

While high-quality recording studio gear cost tens of thousands of dollars decades ago, the equipment listed above could easily be purchased today for a few thousand dollars. Home and amateur recording studios are increasingly common because of the affordability and accessibility of this equipment. The heart of the recording studio is the DAW, which may replicate a DAW found in a music technology classroom, but with the potential for additional gear, more channels, better microphones, and acoustic wall treatments that provide better recordings, if possible. Consult a local audio engineer before designing a recording studio at your school and understand that the size and scope of a recording studio can vary depending on your space and budget. Any traditional classroom may be transformed into a recording studio on a budget with a little elbow grease and imagination.

DIFFERENTIATION

The skills and knowledge required to run live sound and recording sessions may appeal to students who are not drawn to performing with their voice or instruments. By offering opportunities to record sessions or work as a sound engineer for a live performance, students may engage in creative work that is challenging and rewarding, but does not require specific instrumental or vocal technique. Students can participate in live sound and recording projects at a variety of levels, from running cables and setting up gear to producing, editing, and distributing full-length original albums. There is no barrier to participating in these activities and students can choose tasks that best align with their abilities and interests. Student stations in a music technology classroom inherently allow for individualized instruction as students work on independent projects with support and guidance from the facilitator/teacher in the classroom. Students with complementary skill sets may collaborate with one another, working together to produce a better product than a student could complete as an individual.

CONCLUSION

Live sound and recording activities are integral components of every school music program, regardless of style. They are especially critical to students of popular music, as this style is often created in collaborative studio production spaces and is performed in venues with sound systems. Students should have an opportunity to learn principles of sound recording and gain experience engineering live performances, as these skills are essential to the music industry. Whether taught directly through music electives in sound recording, or integrated into ensembles and general music classrooms, a functional knowledge of microphones, cables, connectors, mixers, interfaces, and recording devices will contribute to a comprehensive understanding of this facet of popular music education.

Takeaways

- Dynamic cardioid microphones are extremely versatile and will help to accomplish nearly every live sound and recording objective you may have in your school.
- If possible, use condenser microphones to record acoustic or softer instruments in your classroom. These microphones are more sensitive than dynamic microphones but help to produce a higher quality recording.
- You will need plenty of XLR, mono/TS, and stereo/TRS cables for live performance and recording spaces. Make sure you are using the correct cable for the task; mostly, do not plug in an instrument with a speaker cable.
- Most mixers include some variation of a basic channel strip, so become familiar with its design and features.
- PA systems provide amplification for live performances. A portable all-in-one PA system is affordable and easy to operate.
- Live sound and recording principles may be applied in a variety of classroom spaces, including music technology labs, silent rehearsal spaces, performance venues, and recording studios. Determine which classrooms are most appropriate for your context.
- Roles in live sound and recording provide more opportunities for students, including those who may be less interested in performing with their voice or on an instrument.

Discussion Questions

1. What prior experience do you have with live sound and recording activities? How could these experiences contribute to a child's school music education?
2. Which classroom space appeals most to you as an educator? How would you design this space to fit with your teaching philosophy and goals?
3. Can you identify any potential projects that would require students to apply their knowledge of live sound and recording techniques in an authentic way?

4. How might a knowledge of live sound recording and PAs be useful in working with bands, choirs, orchestras, and general music classes?

Note

1 Clauhs, Franco, and Cremata, "Music Production in School Music Programs," 55–63; and Randles, "Music Teacher as Writer and Producer," 36–52.

PART III

Putting It All Together

OBJECTIVES

- **Compare and contrast** a variety of approaches to creating and performing popular music together as a group.
- **Describe** the role of a teacher as a facilitator.
- **Explain** the role of hip hop in society and school music.
- **Identify** how popular music techniques address National Core Arts Standards for creating music.

Making the Band

The act of making music with others is one of the most powerful experiences for students in a school music program. In popular music education, group music-making can occur in ensembles and technology-based collaborations. While this time may be most productive if students enter the space with a basic understanding of their instruments, voices, and/or digital tools, it is important to provide group experiences early and often. These experiences will motivate students to progress and help foster collaborative skills that are valuable in music and in life. Ensemble experiences in popular music should not mirror existing ensemble experiences in most K-12 schools as it is not always appropriate to apply the standard practices of traditional school music offerings to popular music ensembles and digital collaborations. There is no singular approach to popular music ensemble experiences, and they are largely dependent upon several factors: grade, level of experience, classroom, facilities, resources, and, most importantly, student interest. This chapter recognizes that ensemble experiences can take many forms, and we believe the suggestions outlined here transfer into many popular music teaching contexts.

ACCESS

The first step in designing a popular music ensemble experience is to determine who will participate. While many existing instrumental ensembles have prerequisites (e.g., ability to read traditional music staff notation, prior experience, and formal training), advocates of popular music education insist on minimizing or eliminating these barriers to participation. Each chapter in this volume has emphasized how every instrument and piece of technology has multiple access points and has presented strategies to engage all learners in a meaningful way, regardless of experience or ability. It is possible, for example, for a novice guitar player to play alongside a group of veteran instrumentalists and vocalists, performing an adapted version of the same song using simplified chords. Unlike existing traditional ensembles, popular music groups may be formed with the entire student population in general music classes through the primary grade levels and with any student interested in taking an elective at the secondary level. These collaborations could occur during regularly scheduled music class time and ensemble experiences could be designed as part of normal class instruction. If an elementary school general music teacher has 25 music classes during the course of a week, it is possible that the teacher could have 25 different ensembles, or even smaller ensembles if individual classes were divided into smaller groups; it is simply a matter of mindset.

Ideally, ensemble experiences would occur during the day as part of the school curriculum, and not after school or during other times designated for extracurricular activities. Many students are unable to participate in extracurricular activities because of work schedules, sports, providing childcare for siblings, and other conflicts, and their access to popular music ensembles would be limited by these factors. An extracurricular ensemble also sends a signal that the experience is not a vital part of the school music program. Of course, if an after-school program is the *only* option to start a popular music ensemble, that is certainly better than nothing at all.

Participation in a popular music ensemble should never be dependent upon participation in an existing ensemble. That kind of policy places the values and interests of the music teacher above the interests of the student and is antithetical to the spirit of popular music education. If teachers are worried about future enrollment in existing ensembles, they should make sure those experiences are engaging and relevant to students. Much research to date has indicated that the implementation of popular music ensembles has not detracted from existing school ensembles and has in most cases dramatically increased the level of participation in school music across the board.[1] If secondary school teachers wish to recruit students to participate in an ensemble-based music elective, it should be clear in the course description that no prior experience be required for participation. This policy will attract more students to the school music program and ensure that all students have an opportunity to participate in meaningful music-making experiences.

STARTING A POPULAR MUSIC ENSEMBLE

Coaching versus Directing

The teacher's role in a popular music ensemble or digital collaboration is unlike the director's role in most traditional bands, orchestras, or choirs. A director is typically responsible for choosing repertoire, leading rehearsals, planning concerts, and overseeing the artistic direction of the ensemble. The director is the expert in the room, holds the vision for the final product, and makes most of the decisions about how students should perform the music. This is likely the most efficient model for working with large groups of students and has resulted in professional-level ensembles in the United States that are recognized around the world. However, in popular music settings, the teacher typically serves as a coach or facilitator. The students hold the artistic vision for the group and pick songs, colead rehearsals, and decide how, when, or even if, they wish to share their music with the public. Ideally, the teacher should not appear on stage during performances, allowing the opportunity for students to count off performances, direct themselves, and address the audience.

Instrumentation

There is no standard instrumentation for popular music ensembles and collaborations may use any combinations of instruments and technologies described in Parts I and II of this volume. Instrumentation will be largely dependent upon the musical preferences of the learners and the availability of material resources. Certain instruments do lend themselves to large group instruction, such as the guitar, keyboard, voice, and DAW, and these instruments and technologies are typical of popular music collaborations. Instruction might begin with every student learning a common instrument, or set of common instruments, and then specializing as students are drawn to specific roles in an ensemble. Unlike most band and orchestra programs in which students specialize on one instrument, popular music programs often encourage students to be multi-instrumentalists, developing a proficiency of a variety of instruments and digital tools.

Live horn sections and strings are commonplace in many popular music genres (e.g., funk, R&B, soul, reggae, swing) and students of band and orchestra programs could be included in popular music ensembles and collaborations. Such partnerships will strengthen the school music program and demonstrate how traditional and emerging programs can work together, not in opposition of each other. Students who study improvisation on band and orchestra instruments may provide instrumental solos and all students will likely be able to play written instrumental parts that add texture to a performance. The *Berklee Practice Method: Get Your Band Together*[2] series of method books includes parts for keyboard, guitar, drum kit, electric bass, saxophone, vibraphone, trombone, trumpet, and violin and is designed to help teachers lead an ensemble in the performance of jazz and contemporary music styles. This method may be useful for teachers who wish to combine popular music instruments and traditional band and orchestra instruments together in the same space. This method relies heavily on standard five-line notation, which may or may not be appropriate depending on the context.

Selecting Repertoire

Students should work together, with the director serving as a facilitator, to select repertoire that best aligns with their level of experience and individual musical preferences. Of course, not all students will enjoy the same artists and genres, and this process will involve some compromise. A good question for the teacher to ask their students is, "What songs/artists/bands are you listening to currently?" Their answers might surprise you! Students must also consider what lyrical content is appropriate for their grade level and school. Lyrics that contain misogynistic, violent, and/or drug-related themes are inappropriate for school settings and will threaten the viability of a popular music program. Kidz Bop is a useful resource for selecting repertoire that is age-appropriate for most school settings, and when necessary the lyrics are adjusted to be child-friendly. Another valuable resource is the Little Kids Rock Jamzone, which contains a library of school-appropriate music along with song charts using iconic notation. While performing cover songs is an essential part of learning the language of popular music, the ultimate goal should be for students to create their own original compositions. Visit http://popmusicped.com for links to resources for repertoire.

Practicing Parts

In some regions of the United States, students receive private instruction during the day on a band or orchestra instrument. Ideally, students of popular music instruments would also receive private instruction, but this may not be realistic for many school programs. Most teachers will need to demonstrate instrument techniques and introduce parts to a song in a class-room or ensemble context. In general music classrooms, common practice involves teaching all students a single part on guitar, keyboard, or voice, and then identifying a few students who wish to play bass, drums, or tech-nology. Bass parts may be introduced on the guitar and drum kit parts may be performed first on body percussion. These parts can be practiced by a whole class before a student or group of students select to play these instruments along with the ensemble.

Online resources and mobile apps can be helpful in providing more individualized instruction than may be possible in a classroom or ensemble. Here is a list of valuable resources for learning techniques and songs on a var-iety of instruments:

- *Yousician* (iOS, Android, MacOS, Windows) provides video instruction, iconic notation-based skill-builders, challenges, and popular songs for keyboard, ukulele, guitar, bass, and vocals. Using a game-style format, the program assesses the accuracy of pitch and rhythm, and provides a sequenced pathway of instruction.
- *FourChords* (iOS, Android) provides simplified and advanced chord options for a variety of popular songs on guitar along with video tutorials and adjustable backing tracks.
- *Ultimate Guitar: Chords & Tabs* (iOS, Android, Website) boasts the world's largest catalog of popular music, notated in tablature and chord charts for guitar.
- *Synthesia* (iOS, Android, MacOS, Windows) uses falling notation (similar to Guitar Hero) to teach students how to perform popular songs on the keyboard.
- *Smule* (iOS, Android, Apple TV, tvOS) is a karaoke app that provides iconic notation and lyrics to popular songs. The program provides feed-back about the accuracy of the singer's pitch and note duration.

Visit http://popmusicped.com for an updated list of resources and computer-based tools that may be useful in a popular music classroom. Another valuable resource for learning parts is YouTube, as many YouTube creators have channels dedicated to teaching songs for ukulele, keyboard, guitar, bass, and drums as well as karaoke tracks for popular songs.

ENSEMBLE APPROACHES

Informal Learning

Informal learning is a theory of teaching music based on the research of Lucy Green, who wrote the following in her book *How Popular Musicians Learn*:

> young musicians largely teach themselves or "pick up" skills and knowledge, usually with the help or encouragement of their family and peers, by watching and imitating musicians around them and by making reference to recordings or performances and other live events involving their chosen music.[3]

The theory of informal learning presented in this book inspired many music teacher educators to consider the mismatch between school music and students' music, both in content and process. Daniel Isbell, a professor of music education at Louisiana State University, explains that informal learning requires that "teachers function more as facilitators and guides for students who are allowed opportunities to enter the educational setting at any time, explore topics immediately of interest to them, and contribute to the path of instruction."[4] The work also serves a pedagogical foundation for a nonprofit organization based in the UK called Musical Futures, which has trained teachers and launched popular music programs in over a thousand secondary schools.[5] It should be noted that activities fall on an informal/formal spectrum. There are elements of formality in popular music facilitation just as there are elements of informality in some aspects of classical training.

Visit www.musicalfutures.org/ for more information about the Musical Futures organization and informal learning.

Modern Band

One of the most significant movements in American music education over the past decade may be the adoption of **modern band** programs in the largest school districts across the United States. The movement was sparked and fueled by the nonprofit organization Little Kids Rock, who has delivered instruments and training to help reach more than a million students at the time of this publication. Modern bands are guided by a student-centered repertoire and a flexible instrumentation that often includes – but is not limited to – guitar, bass, keyboard, drums, vocals, and technology.[6]

> ### ▶ 2019 NHE MODERN BAND AUDITION REQUIREMENTS
>
> In 2019, NAfME included modern band as an all-national honor ensemble (along with concert band, jazz band, symphony orchestra, mixed choir, and guitar ensemble) at the annual conference in Orlando, Florida, validating this kind of band as a standard school ensemble. The audition requirements for the inaugural all-national modern band were created by the ensemble facilitator Scott Burstein and made available to the public through the NAfME website at https://nafme.org/programs/all-national-honor-ensembles/. While these audition requirements may be helpful to secondary school programs that wish to include modern band alongside other auditioned groups (e.g., jazz band, show choir) or counties and state associations that wish to include modern band honor ensembles, it is important to note that modern band is typically taught by elementary and secondary general music teachers to all students in the school population. Accessibility and inclusion are important aims of popular music education, so nonauditioned modern band opportunities should be available to every student.
>
> ### 2019 NHE Modern Band Audition Requirements
>
> Due to the nature of the ensemble, all students are required to demonstrate facility on a variety of styles. These styles can include Pop, Rock, Hip Hop, R&B, Country, Metal, or other genres. While singing is not mandatory for instrument auditionees, preparation of a short excerpt demonstrating singing ability is recommended.
>
> **Vocals/Rap:** Two prepared songs of contrasting style performed with instrument track (no sing-alongs) or live ensemble.
>
> - One piece should demonstrate background vocals or ability to sing harmonies.
> - The other piece should include improvisation.
> - One of the pieces can be original, the other must be a cover.
> - Rapping highly encouraged, either as a cover or original.
>
> **Guitar:** Two prepared songs of contrasting style. Can be excerpt of longer piece, but should show diversity of both rhythmic and melodic playing.
>
> - One piece must include a lead guitar solo. Examples would include solos by Jimi Hendrix, Carlos Santana, David Gilmour, Slash, Stevie Ray Vaughn, etc.
> - Both pieces should demonstrate variety of chordal usage: open chords, barre chords, power chords, triads, etc.
>
> **Bass:** Four prepared bass grooves.
>
> - Should demonstrate a variety of styles that show versatility and ability to play in the pocket.

- Recommended bassists for cover grooves: James Jamerson, Carol Kaye, Flea, Paul McCartney, John Entwistle, etc.
- One can be composed, three must be covers.

Drums: Two prepared pieces with multiple patterns in each.

- Should demonstrate a variety of groove styles: aka Rock, Hip Hop, Latin, etc.
- Must demonstrate ability to play along with recording and switch between drum grooves in sections of the song.

Other Instruments (ukulele, brass, strings, winds, etc.): Two prepared pieces that demonstrate style and versality as lead or accompanist. Should include improvisatory section.

For teachers who are working with full modern bands that include guitars, bass, drums, keys, and vocals, there are often various instrumentation options available. If you are using multiple drum kits, it is best to position the drum kits in the center of the room close together. Separating drummers to the periphery of the ensemble makes it difficult to lock into a groove. The guitarists and keyboard players in a modern band will often be grouped together for ease of instruction, although they don't need to be next to each other when it is time for a performance. The stage plot in Figure 12.1 can help with the organization of instrumentalists on the stage and in the classroom.

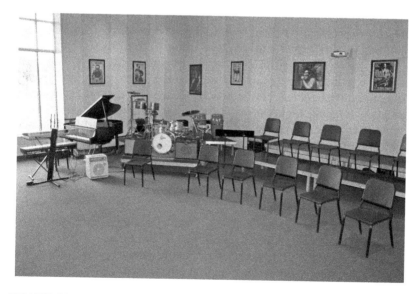

FIGURE 12.1
Sample Popular Music Ensemble Setup
Photo courtesy of Steve Holley

Berklee Method

The Berklee College of Music was one of the first, and is certainly one of the most prominent, institutions of popular music education in the United States. The college has developed, codified, and standardized an approach to leading ensembles over several decades and their model may be useful to secondary schools interested in designing a comprehensive popular music program. Of course, this model may be adapted to fit the context specific needs and resources available at any given school. The Berklee model for teaching guitar, bass, drums, and keyboard follows a four-tiered system:

1. *Performance and lecture*: teachers perform these instruments and discuss how their parts fit together (as an alternative, teachers could play recordings of ensembles and discuss instrument-specific roles).
2. *Sections*: players of similar instruments learn their parts as a group (e.g., group lesson).
3. *Guided rehearsals*: coached by an instructor working on an arrangement.
4. *Independent rehearsals*: bands meet without a teacher and develop their ensemble playing on their own.[7]

See the "Berklee Practice Method Teacher's Guide" by Matt Marvuglio and Jonathan Feist for more information about this four-tiered approach to popular music ensembles.

Hybrid Spaces

Music education scholar Evan Tobias charged music teachers to consider how to engage students with multiple musical interests and skill sets – or in his words, hyphenated musicians – in classrooms that provide multiple avenues for creative expression – hybrid spaces. A hyphenated musician may be any combination of performer (on acoustic and/or electronic instruments and vocals), recording engineer, producer, and mixing engineer, serving as multiple roles in a hybrid space, which includes the instruments and technologies to make this possible.[8] This viewpoint recognizes that students are often interested in learning multiple instruments and acquiring a variety of skill sets. Music teachers can create **hybrid ensembles** (also called flexible or flex ensembles) that could accommodate both traditional instruments in the band and orchestra alongside emerging instruments and technologies, allowing for unique collaborations that push the boundaries of school music.

Virtual Ensemble

A **virtual ensemble** is a group whose performances are created through the layering of audio and/or video recordings.[9] The number of participants in this ensemble experience may range from one person, who records themselves multiple times to create an ensemble sound (search YouTube for Jacob Collier), to thousands of participants across hundreds of countries, who contribute recordings of themselves to be layered and combined for an ensemble sound (search YouTube for Eric Whitacre's virtual choir). The possibilities for virtual ensemble experiences are limitless and can be tailored to the individual learning goals of the student. Some apps for mobile devices make virtual ensemble experiences easy to facilitate, including acappella (iOS and Android) which allows users to video record and layer multiple tracks of themselves singing or playing parts to a song.

SUGGESTED RESOURCE

Coaching a Popular Music Ensemble (2019) by Grammy-nominated music educator Steve Holley is a valuable resource on approaches and methods for creating learner-centered rehearsals. Visit http://steveholleymusic.com for more information.

STAGE PRESENCE

No matter which approach, or blend of approaches, is most appropriate for your school and students, the success of a performance depends largely on the stage presence of the group. This section examines how students in various roles of a popular music ensemble – lead singer, backing vocalists, and instrumentalists – elevate a performance through stage presence techniques.

Lead Singer

Simply put, a lead singer is the vocalist who sings the melody and is the focus of the audience's attention. Often, lead singers stand in front of other musicians who provide support on instruments and background vocals, although the lead singer may play an instrument as well. Many school ensembles utilize multiple lead singers, taking turns within songs or throughout a performance, to engage more students in this role. The lead singer is the front person who must interpret the lyrics to tell a story. Lead singers are expected to have charisma and confidence as a performer, all with their own appeal and personality. A lead singer does not need to be a great dancer to engage their audience, although all singers should be able to move expressively. Another important aspect of being a good lead singer is communicating with the band about when to slow down, speed up, or stop the music, using subtle cues that are integrated into the performance.

LEADING THE BAND

Here are standard cues lead singers can use to communicate with the band:[10]

- Gentle hand gestures downwards – less volume.
- Raised fist – indicates "watch for ending."
- Same fist dropped down sharply – STOP.
- Arm circling – repeat the previous passage.

A lead singer is also expected to communicate with the audience throughout the performance. This includes introducing the band, announcing songs, and building a rapport with the audience. A good lead singer comes across as confident and sincere. If your student does not have much confidence or experience in performing in front of an audience as a lead singer, consider writing some notes and practice these during each rehearsal.

Storytelling
A lead singer is a storyteller. Lead singers need to believe the story they are telling and to share that belief with the audience. It is essential for the lead singer (and all singers in the band) to understand the complexities of the lyrics so that they can present them in a stimulating and connective way to the audience, through emotive singing and physical movement.

IT'S ALL ABOUT THE STORY: SUGGESTED ACTIVITY

The following exercises will help students connect with song lyrics and prepare them to tell a story.

Acting the Lyrics
1. Students should select a song that they like and that is appropriate for the band.
2. Students read through the lyrics silently, being mindful of the story line.
3. Singers take turns reading the verse of the lyrics to one another as though this is the most exciting or dramatic story they have ever read. They should use the whole body to tell the story to one another.

Physical Expression of the Lyrics
1. Following the same procedures above, students: select a song, print the words, and read the lyrics silently.
2. Divide students into pairs and have them act out the lyrics as if they were playing charades. They should make thoughtful choices about how they would explain the meaning of the lines without being able to say the words aloud.
3. Students play and sing through the song incorporating the physical gestures they created.

Backing Vocalists
Backing vocalists provide vocal harmonies and countermelodies that support the lead vocal. These vocalists may also take turns rotating into the role of lead singer, if you wish to provide more students with the experience of leading a band. Backing vocalists may use choreography, even a simple rock step (also

called touch step), in which students transfer their weight from one foot to another in time with the music, to add visual interest to a performance. Simple arm movements or finger snapping are subtle gestures that make a big difference as well.

Instrumentalists

Instrumentalists are comprised of rhythm section players (e.g., keyboard, guitar, bass, drums, percussion), horns (e.g., trumpet, saxophone, trombone), and/or strings. They provide the accompaniment to support the vocal melody or all parts of a song that have no vocals (e.g., an instrumental), and may be featured as individual soloists, performing improvised or composed melodies during solo sections. Much like backing vocalists, instrumentalists can command stage presence through simple choreography (e.g., rock step, horn flashes) and/or moving an instrument from side to side in time with the music. It is most effective to reserve these movements for special parts of the song, such as the chorus or instrumental interlude, to maximize the effect of the gesture.

Image

One of the main ways to display image is through the selection of the clothes students choose to wear. When working with other musicians as a unit, what students wear and how they present themselves should reflect the style of music they play.[11] For instance, a rock band wearing formal attire is unlikely to be taken seriously unless the effect is meant for novelty value. Students' clothes should not restrict their breathing, playing, or movement and should be appropriate for school settings.

DIFFERENTIATION

Students of different instruments and musical backgrounds may bring divergent skill sets to the ensemble setting. Some students may have learned to play their instrument primarily by ear while others may have had years of formal training reading standard notation. Experience levels with improvisation and composition may also vary. The teacher/facilitator of the ensemble must negotiate these differences and provide learning experiences that celebrate students' strengths while challenging them to progress in weaker areas. When learning new songs or skills, teachers should engage multiple modes of learning – by ear, through iconic notation, and traditional staff notation – when it seems appropriate for the student or context, apprenticeship, and guided practice.

CONCLUSION

Popular music ensemble experiences and digital collaborations should be driven by student interest and reflective of the goals and aspirations of all learners in the school community. The strongest music programs may be the ones that include collaborations among traditional and emerging ensembles, providing complementary skill sets to the greatest number of students. Popular music ensembles are typically led by students and facilitated by teachers, a mindset that may be unfamiliar, and potentially uncomfortable, for many music teachers. If properly structured, an autonomous student-led popular music ensemble can be an incredibly rewarding experience for everyone involved and help to develop leadership and collaboration skills that last a lifetime. It requires commitment, trust, and patience, but is well worth the effort.

Takeaways

- Student voice and choice play an important role in the development of popular music ensembles.
- All students should have access to a range of ensembles and music collaborations.
- There are a variety of approaches to making popular music ensembles.
- Teachers function as facilitators, not directors, in popular music ensembles.

Discussion Questions

1. Which approach to making ensembles appeals most to you and why?
2. Have you participated in a class or ensemble where the teacher served as a facilitator? What was rewarding or challenging about this experience?
3. What collaborative activities or projects can you imagine for a band, orchestra, and choir in partnership with a popular music ensemble?

Notes

1 Clauhs and Cremata, "Student Voice and Choice," 101–16; Powell, "Student Enrollment in Traditional Music Ensembles," 20–23.
2 Marvuglio and Feist, *Berklee Practice Method*.
3 Green, *How Popular Musicians Learn*.
4 Isbell, "Professional Development in the United Kingdom," 39–58.
5 Hallam and Creech, *Music Education in the 21st Century in the United Kingdom*.
6 Powell and Burstein, "Popular Music and Modern Band Principles," 244–45.
7 Marvuglio and Feist, *Berklee Practice Method*.
8 Tobias, "Songwriting and Technology Course," 329–46.
9 Cayari, "Virtual Vocal Ensembles."
10 "Role of the Lead Vocalist."
11 Ibid.

Songwriting, Improvisation, and Arranging

Creative activities such as songwriting, improvisation, and arranging are essential components of a popular music curriculum. These experiences balance the recreative focus of most traditional school music programs and are aligned with many of the 2014 National Core Arts Standards driven by *creating* music.[1] Although there are an increasing number of resources that focus on composing in bands, choirs, and orchestras,[2] most traditional ensembles typically perform other composers' works, which may be the most appropriate goal considering the size, structure, and function of these groups. With this in mind, we will explore some ways to introduce songwriting, improvisation, and arranging into popular music ensembles and classes in this chapter. Students do not need a formal understanding of melody, harmony, and part-writing rules to write songs, arrange, or improvise. Students have a lifetime of experience listening to music, and through an asset-based model of instruction that recognizes the strengths they bring to school, this chapter presents several approaches to involve students in creative music-making experiences right away.

> Students only need to know one chord to begin songwriting exercises with a guitar, ukulele, or keyboard. Visit http://popmusicped.com for examples of famous one-chord songs.

SONGWRITING

Parody

A **parody** is a song that uses the same chords, structure, and melody as an existing song, but replaces the text with original lyrics. Weird Al Yankovic is famous for his humorous parodies of popular songs. Using parody as a songwriting technique helps students to focus on lyric writing, since the chord progression and the melody are provided by the original song. Having students write new lyrics to a familiar song is a good place to start with songwriting. A parody could explore topics from academic subjects leading toward inter-disciplinary learning, or draw inspiration from art, photographs, stories, and everyday experiences in the students' own lives.

Familiar Chord Progressions

There are common **chord progressions** found in hundreds, if not thousands, of familiar songs (e.g., I–IV–V, I–V–vi–IV, blues progressions). The comedy group Axis of Awesome famously performed a "Four Chord Song" which demonstrated how many popular songs use the I–V–vi–IV chord progression.[3] On guitar, the easiest way to play this progression is in the key of G:

G	D	E mi	C
(I	V	vi	IV)

On the ukulele and piano, the easiest way to play this progression is in the key of C:

C	G	A mi	F
(I	V	vi	IV)

There are thousands of songs that use a I–V–vi–IV progression or a variation of the progression starting on the vi for a minor key: vi–IV–I–V. The same chords may also be rearranged to produce another common chord progression: IV–I–vi–V.

Mixing Up Chords

The chords within these familiar chord progressions work well with one another, in any order. The reality is that you can take any chord progression from any song, mix up the chords in any order that you want, and that new progression will still sound pretty great! Students can mix and match a variety of diatonic chords to discover new progressions. They can experiment by moving vertically, horizontally, or diagonally in any direction along the tic-tac-toe diatonic chord chart in Figure 13.1.

Using Visuals or Written Prompts

Students may struggle to generate original material for a song, especially if they are in a group. One student might want to write about their summer break while another student wants to write about their favorite sports team. Providing students with a visual image or a written prompt can give them the inspiration to get started. Students can also choose their own meaningful images from the photos on their phone or a quick Google search. If a picture

C	Dmi	Emi
F	G	Ami
Ami	C	F

C	Dmi	Emi
F	G	Ami
Ami	C	F

C	Dmi	Emi
F	G	Ami
Ami	C	F

FIGURE 13.1
Chord Tic-Tac-Toe

FIGURE 13.2
Public Domain Images from unsplash.com

is worth a thousand words, it certainly can be worth a few songs! The best pictures to use are ones that are open to interpretation or might inspire new ideas. The images in Figure 13.2 are examples of public domain photographs from unsplash.com that students can use as inspiration for new songs.

When using written prompts, it is a good idea to use prompts that may be interpreted in several different ways. For example: "I hope you are happy," "No, I'm not sorry," or "Well, that's a surprise!" can be interpreted many ways to inspire creativity from a variety of angles.

Lyric Writing

One approach to lyric writing is to develop a list of words or expressions that connect to a topic. Students can choose a topic of their own, drawing inspiration from a photo, cartoon, piece of art, or any other relevant source.

Example topic: Chapter 13
Brainstorming words: songwriting, improvisation, arranging, create, standards, beat, rhyme

After brainstorming words, students identify potential rhyme pairs to match the words related to their topic. The rhyme does not need to be the same number of syllables as the original word. It may be helpful to start at the beginning of the alphabet and carefully consider the possibilities. Online rhyming dictionaries are an invaluable resource for this activity. Of course, some brainstorming words (e.g., beat) will yield more rhymes than others (e.g., standards).

Brainstorming word (A): rhyme
Rhyming words (A): climb, chime, sublime, time, anytime, slime, crime, prime
Brainstorming word (B): beat
Rhyming words (B): complete, feet, street, meat, heat, eat, concrete, seat, defeat, discrete

These rhyme pairs can be organized into a scheme by placing them at the end of each line. In Rhyme Scheme Example 1 and 2, the letter "A" indicates the first rhyme pair for "rhyme," the letter "B" indicates a second rhyme pair for "beat."

Rhyme Scheme Example 1:

1. rhyme (A)
2. time (A)
3. beat (B)
4. feet (B)

Rhyme Scheme Example 2:

1. rhyme (A)
2. beat (B)
3. time (A)
4. feet (B)

Finally, students develop a phrase that completes each line. It is useful to complete this step with a backing track so they can determine how the phrase aligns with the tempo, style, key, and feel of the instrumental parts.

Completed Verse:

1. It is easy to make a rhyme   (A)
2. You can do it any time   (A)
3. Just write along to a beat   (B)
4. Turn up the mic and move your feet   (B)

Writing Melodies

After developing lyrics that match the rhythm and feel of their song, students may consider writing a melody. If they are interested in writing in the style of hip hop, some or all the lyrics may be rapped and not sung. Students should not be required to write a melody if it does not fit the style of their song. Guitars,

FIGURE 13.3

A Virtual Instrument Limited to the C Major Scale in GarageBand for iOS
Screenshot reprinted with permission from Apple Inc

keyboards, and other melodic instruments, including virtual software tools, can be useful devices to help students identify melodies that work with their lyrics and chord progressions. For simple diatonic chord progressions, it may be useful to have students limit their note choices to a single major or minor scale. The virtual instruments included on the iOS version of GarageBand allow the user to limit note choices for guitar, bass, and keyboard. This may be a useful tool, particularly for students who do not play these instruments (Figure 13.3).

IMPROVISATION

As demonstrated in the instrumental chapters throughout this book, soloing and improvisation are activities for all students, not just the "best" or most accomplished musicians. It is critical that students experience success early and often with improvisation so that they feel encouraged to create music throughout their lives without fear of failure. By starting gradually with one-note solos, and then two-note solos, students can build their confidence over time. Once students feel comfortable with four-note solos, they can learn pentatonic shapes on fretted instruments, or use Jam Cards[4] to learn

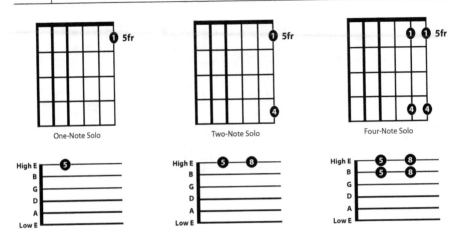

FIGURE 13.4
Soloing with One to Four Notes

pentatonic scales on the keyboard. Students can use the same pattern/shape up and down the fretboard or keyboard to play the scale in each key. And this concept works with major and minor scales, as well as scales in all modes. One shape can unlock a scale in any key!

One-, Two-, and Four-Note Solos

Students (and teachers) will be more comfortable improvising in a supportive environment that celebrates early success. An activity using one-, two-, and four-note solos, is a low-stress approach to introducing improvisation.

> Visit http://popmusicped.com for links to backing tracks in A minor to play while students practice solos for four beats. When a student's four beats are up, immediately move to the next student without a break.

This approach allows several students to improvise solos in a relatively short amount of time. The examples in Figure 13.4 indicate which notes to play for a one-, two-, and four-note guitar solo in the key of A minor.

Jam Cards

As mentioned in Chapter 6, Little Kids Rock developed Jam Cards to help students find their place on a keyboard (Figure 13.5). Scale-based Jam Cards, which include pentatonic, blues, major, and minor scales, are useful tools for introducing improvisation on this instrument. Students can slide the Jam Card behind the keyboard and immediately identify note choices for improvisation. Keyboard students could place this card so that the root note is "A," and

FIGURE 13.5
Jam Card for the Minor Pentatonic Scale
Image courtesy of Little Kids Rock

improvise together with guitar players that are using the chord diagrams in Figure 13.3 along with an A minor play-along track.

ARRANGING

Creating Song Arrangements

The small size and democratic nature of popular music ensembles make them well-suited for arranging activities. If the ensemble is covering a song, students can listen to an original recording and make decisions about strumming patterns, instrumentation, and song form. Unlike most school music ensembles in which the teacher typically buys arrangements without much student input, popular music ensembles challenge students to take an active role in making musical decisions about arranging songs. There are several factors to think through as your students prepare to arrange music for the ensemble, including key signature, form, style, instrumentation, and solo sections.

Key Signature

There are multiple reasons why students might want to change the key signature of a song. One reason is to put the song in a key where they best know how to play the chords. A song in the key of F has a B♭ for the IV chord, and a Dmi chord as the vi chord. Since B♭ and Dmi are chords that can be challenging to play for beginners, students might consider raising the song a whole step to the key of G, so that the IV chord is C and the vi chord is an E minor.

I–V–iv–IV CHORD PROGRESSION

Original key of F = F–C–Dmi–B♭
New, easier key of G = G–D–Emi–C

Another reason students might want to change the key of a song is to put the song in a more comfortable vocal range. Especially with younger students, it is important to sing in ranges that are developmentally appropriate for a child's voice. Since many rock songs include vocal belting or singing in extended vocal ranges, it is important to protect young voices and change the key of the song when needed. When in doubt, the key of D is usually a good one for younger students. One additional reason to change the key of a song is if the ensemble is doing a "mash-up" of two songs. Being able to switch between the songs, or even play parts of both songs at the same time (counterpoint), works best if students are not changing keys as the songs change.

Form

Unlike most pieces of music for bands, choirs, and orchestras, popular music ensembles often perform sections of songs, but do not always perform the whole song. Some songs have long instrumental breakdowns, or bridge sections that introduce new chords. Students and teachers can discuss which sections of a song to perform and which sections to leave out. There are no rules that state all the verses of a song must be performed. Students should feel free to pick and choose the section of the song that works best for the ensemble and performance context.

Style

Another option for arranging a song is to switch up the style of a song. For example, students can take a fast-paced rock song and create a mellow acoustic guitar or ukulele version, or a mellow slow song like Bob Marley's "Three Little Birds" can be rearranged with a rock style that includes electric guitars and drum kit. Mixing up the styles of the songs can be a fun way to add additional elements of student choice when it comes to the arrangement of the songs.

Instrumentation

If the ensemble does not have all the instruments to cover a song, it is a great opportunity to recreate sounds on synthesizers and iPads. Remember that most keyboards have synthesized sounds that can replicate horns, strings, or drum machines. Likewise, using technology such as the iPad in your ensemble can allow you to incorporate a variety of timbres into the songs.

Solo Sections

As students arrange songs for a popular music ensemble, adding in solo breaks is a great way to feature several members of the group. And remember, some of the best solos are very simple! Encourage students to start with a one-, two-, or four-note solo and work their way up from there.

CONCLUSION

Songwriting, improvisation, and arranging are essential components of popular music ensembles and classes. Encouraging students to be songwriters from an early age is easy through scaffolding approaches that provide the support needed for students to find success. Parodies, mixing up chords, lyric writing activities, and visual and written prompts can provide the inspiration needed for students to experience success in songwriting. Similarly, scaffolding approaches to facilitate improvisation in a safe space will foster opportunities for student success. As the teacher, you and your students have options about arranging songs and transposing songs into keys that are appropriate for their skill level and vocal health.

Takeaways

- There are many ways to incorporate songwriting into the classroom. The key is to set the students up for success through structured activities.
- All students should solo and improvise when playing popular music instruments, not just the most talented ones. Start with simple one- and two-note solos to set your students up for success.
- Changing the key of a song can put the song into a friendlier key for beginning instrumentalists and can also accommodate the vocal ranges of your students.

Discussion Questions

1. Do you remember your first experience with soloing or improvising in front of other people? How are the approaches described in this chapter similar or different from your experience?
2. Do you consider yourself a songwriter? Is it important for the teacher to be a songwriter if they are going to ask their students to write songs? Why or why not?
3. What are some of the challenges that you anticipate in arranging music for popular music ensembles?

Notes

1 NAfME, "Standards."
2 Kerchner and Strand, *Composing in Choir*; and Randles and Stringham, *Composing in Band and Orchestra.*
3 Axis of Awesome, "Four Chord Song."
4 Wish et al., *Modern Band Movement.*

Hip Hop

In Chapter 1, we defined popular music as the music listened to, shared, emulated, and created by young people. Popular music pedagogies have traditionally focused on the musical goals of the learner, therefore the music preferences and aspirations of students should be prioritized in a school popular music program. Although many popular music education movements in the UK and the United States initially began with teaching and learning rock, popular music is certainly not synonymous with rock music and is ever-changing, varying widely by geographic location, student population, and place in time. And while informal music learning pioneer and scholar Lucy Green's research has been used extensively to inform popular music programs around the world, she intentionally excluded styles and approaches to learning music that were electronic-based from her research because they "contain significant differences from those of guitar-based rock."[1]

According to a Nielsen Music year-end report in 2017, hip hop and R&B surpassed rock as the most widely consumed musical genres in the United States,[2] so it is likely that many students in K-12 school settings across the United States prefer these styles of music. Simply put, hip hop is the most popular form of popular music. Considering the cultural importance of music and the associations between genres and socially constructed races/ethnicities, educators should be especially careful not to promote styles of music incongruent with the preferences of their students. Music education scholar Juliet Hess cautions that while "popular music education proponents often assume that popular music relates to students' realities, in actuality, popular music education sometimes involves imposing music from 1960s and 1970s rock genres – music rooted in specific raced, classed, gendered, and sexual identities."[3] Music teachers who blindly introduce rock band programs and repertoire without considering the voice of their students may be replicating hegemonic structures in school music programs instead of replacing them. To avoid this, educators should consider how the voice of their students can play a role in shaping the school music curriculum.[4]

Cultural appropriation is the act of a person or group from one culture adopting a tradition or expression from another culture as their own. Examples of appropriation in popular music include Katy Perry dressing up as an Egyptian pharaoh in her music video for Dark Horse[5] or Iggy Azalea using a stereotypically African American "accent" when rapping.[6] There are many examples of appropriation in school music education as well. The adoption of historically African American art forms such as jazz, blues, hip hop, and R&B in predominantly white school music programs may arguably be a form of appropriation, especially if these styles are not studied within the proper context and given the same degree of respect as Western European classical traditions. Scholar Patricia Shehan Campbell advises "because schools operate within societies that prize cultural democracy, their curricular subjects for study, including music, are intended to be taught and learned from the perspective of more than a single dominant culture."[7]

It would also be wrong to assume that students of a dominant culture do not already engage with music strongly associated with nondominant cultures. A large share of the hip hop market is white listeners, particularly between the ages of 18 and 34.[8] If hip hop is the musical preference of students in a classroom, then a responsive popular music educator should engage with that style, but do so with care and context. Educators should be sure that students treat all musical genres with respect and understand the origins and social context of a variety of songs and styles. Sensitivity to culture and tradition may help minimize the risk of appropriation in a popular music classroom.

BASICS

Hip hop is a culture and art/music movement that came out of the South Bronx in the late 1970s. In reference to music, the term "hip hop music" is sometimes used interchangeably with "rap music," although hip hop is inclusive of more than just rapping. There are four recognized elements of hip hop. These elements include MCing/emceeing (or rapping), DJing/deejaying or "turntabling," breakdancing, and graffiti.[9] In recent years, some artists and scholars have added other elements to be considered, including knowledge of self/consciousness, beatboxing, and fashion, among others.

While it is important to understand the role of breakdancing and graffiti in hip hop culture, this chapter will focus on the elements of MCing/emceeing and DJing/deejaying. In the early years of hip hop, the disc jockey, or **DJ/deejay**, would spin records often switching back and forth between two records at the same time. The instrumental breaks of the songs often elicited the strongest reaction from the audience. The DJ would then switch back and forth between the records to extend the break section. The dancers who would dance over the breaks (breakdancing) became known as "break boys" and "break girls," which we now refer to as "b-boys and b-girls."

As the popularity of DJing dance parties grew in the South Bronx in the late 1970s, DJs would start to talk over the music to make announcements and give shout-outs to people in the room. Talking on the mic over the music created a need for a Master of Ceremonies (**MC/emcee**). The MC would often speak short rhyming tags to promote the DJ, and those shorter rhymes turned into longer rhymes and stories. These longer rhymes were spoken (rapped) over the break beats of songs, thus giving birth to the genre of rap music.

APPROACHES

There are many ways to engage students with hip hop culture and rap music. Curated databases such as hiphoped.com and http://hiphoparchive.org/ have a number of resource that are useful in a popular music education classroom. Visit http://popmusicped.com for direct links to these resources and more.

Making Beats
By focusing on the role of the DJ and the MC, students can create their own break beats and rap songs. One way to "make beats" is to use a free, online-based beat sequencer. Figure 14.1 illustrates the backbeat from Chapter 7, which can easily be replicated by online sequencers, such as drumbit or Splice Beat Baker (Figure 14.2). Once students understand how to build the backbeat on a **drum sequencer**, they can add instruments, or even change the sounds that the kick and snare drums make. Most DAWs also have beat sequencers built in that allow users to customize the sounds and timings of the beat with almost unlimited possibilities.

Lyric Writing
Chapter 13 provided a variety of songwriting and lyric writing activities that may be useful for creating songs in the style of hip hop. Be sure to review those activities as you consider how to include lyric writing for rap songs as part of songwriting activities. Lyric writing for hip hop songs not only brings elements of creating into the music classroom, but it is also consistent with authentic approaches to rapping. Within the hip hop community, writing original rhymes and lyrics is the focal point of song creation. Rappers will almost never cover a song written by another rapper; the focus is always on

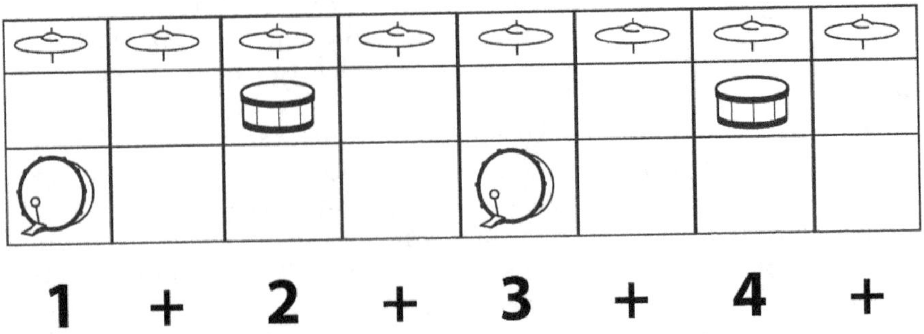

FIGURE 14.1
Rock Beat Rhythm on Drum Kit

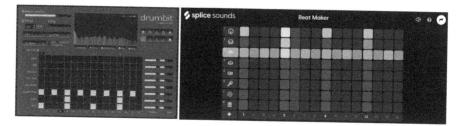

FIGURE 14.2
Rock Beat Rhythm on drumbit and Splice Beatmaker

creating new art, not replicating what already exists. In fact, accusing someone of having a "ghostwriter" is a significant criticism in the rap community.

Students can learn to write their own original lyrics in an activity called Hip Hop Hamburger.[10] Student MCs create rhyming couplets to sing a hook or chorus section (the bun) and rap a verse (the meat). These sections could use a variety of rhyming forms including AABB, ABAB, or AAAA. After the verse, the hook section returns at the end and is a repeat of the top section (Figure 14.3).

Slogans

Improvisation is an essential element of hip hop and the art of freestyling is sometimes compared to the act of taking a jazz solo. MCs borrow language from others and rely on patterns and other devices when performing a freestyle rap. Groups of MCs join together in a rap **cypher** to freestyle together, much like a jam session in the jazz tradition. Students can practice improvising in their own cyphers using one device called a **slogan**. A slogan (or catch phrase) is a short expression placed at the end of each improvised line. The following example uses the address of our website to illustrate this concept.

> Videos for you to see, popmusicped.com.
> Demos and activities, popmusicped.com.
> Drums, bass, vocals, keys, popmusicped.com.
> Ensembles and technologies, popmusicped.com.

In addition to shamelessly promoting the website resource, this slogan-based freestyle verse serves to inform the listener about a topic. Students can create slogans that are about themselves, the school, an event, or anything relevant to their lives.

DIFFERENTIATION

There are many opportunities for differentiation and scaffolding within lyric writing activities. Beginning students can simply follow prescriptive outlines over a backing track to get the feel for rapping to a beat.

Name_____ Group Members _____

Topic:_____

TOP BUN: Hook/Chorus, 4 measures (A section)

A _____

A_____

B_____

B_____

MEAT/CHEESE: Rap/Verse, 8 measures (B section)

A _____

A_____

B_____

B_____

A _____

A_____

B_____

B_____

BOTTOM BUN: Hook/Chorus, 4 measures (A section)

A _____

A_____

B_____

B_____

FIGURE 14.3
Lyric Writing Template
Image courtesy of Little Kids Rock

My name is _____
And I'm from _____
And my favorite color is _____

More advanced students can create their own raps using end-rhyme words at the end of each sentence.

I like to rap on the beat
I think my flow is neat

You should get out of your seat
So we can get something to eat

As students feel comfortable creating their own rhymes, they can use different rhythmic structures such as a triplet and sixteenth notes to deliver their rhymes. Less experienced students might develop their songs using preexisting backing tracks while more experienced students should create their own beats using DAWs and sequencers.

CONCLUSION

This chapter critiqued the notion of a singular "pedagogy" for a topic as expansive and ever-changing as popular music. Inspired by the groundbreaking work of Lucy Green, many educators and some scholars extrapolated the learning approaches of a single case of rock musicians to an entire field of popular music pedagogy. Although Green's work[11] illuminated how some popular musicians learn, it certainly did not – nor did it intend to – describe how all popular musicians learn. In this chapter, we emphasized modes of learning unique to the performance of hip hop – the most widely consumed form of music in the United States.

While the lyrical content of rap and hip hop have experienced a disproportionate amount of criticism (and much of the content that currently exists is an exploitation of black artists by white producers), there are examples of sexist, misogynistic, homophobic, and racist lyrics in virtually every style of music. Music educators might choose to avoid lyrics that promote these themes altogether, or critically examine lyrics with their students to build understanding and positively influence listening habits outside of the classroom. That choice may depend upon the age of the student and the experience of the teacher. Either way, teachers should facilitate lyric writing and songwriting activities that promote self-expression, empathy, justice, and counternarratives of the news and media. Through these efforts, popular music pedagogies provide, as Sheila Woodward writes, an opportunity to promote social change and offer a "critical narrative of society."[12]

Takeaways

- Popular music education is not limited to rock styles and garage bands.
- The most widely consumed music styles in the United States are currently hip hop and R&B.
- Sensitivity to culture and tradition may help minimize the risk of appropriation in a popular music classroom.

Discussion Questions

1. What support/resources do you need to feel confident about teaching the musical preferences of your students?
2. What examples of cultural appropriation do you see in schools and the music industry today?

3. What strategies could be used to provide context to musical traditions associated with cultures that may or may not be represented in your classroom?

Notes

1 Green, "Music Educators Learn from Popular Musicians," 225–41.
2 Serjeant, "Hip Hop and R&B Surpass Rock."
3 Hess, "A Way Forward or a New Hegemony?" 30.
4 Clauhs and Cremata, "Student Voice and Choice," 101–16.
5 Pennington, "Dissolving the Other," 111–27.
6 Guo, "How Iggy Azalea Mastered Her 'Blaccent'."
7 Campbell, *Teaching Music Globally*, 12.
8 RBR-TVBR, "Hip-Hop, Consumers and Retail."
9 Chang, *Can't Stop Won't Stop*.
10 Wish et al., "Hip Hop Hamburger."
11 Green, *How Popular Musicians Learn*.
12 Woodward, "Social Justice and Popular Music Education," 395–411.

GLOSSARY

3:1 rule: The distance between two microphones should be at least three times greater than the distance from the microphone to the source of the sound.

Attenuate: To reduce in sound. Sometimes used to describe the decay of a wave form (as in attenuation).

Audio interface: A device that translates audible sounds into digital information and vice versa.

Audio: Any sound recorded with a microphone, acoustic instrument, or electric instrument, typically through a cable with an XLR or 1/4 connector.

Aux sends: The send knobs on a channel strip control how much of the signal is processed by reverb, delay, chorus, or other effects.

Backbeat: A common rhythmic pattern in popular music in which the snare drum sounds on beats 2 and 4.

Backing track: A recorded musical accompaniment.

Barre chord: Using one finger (typically the pointer finger) across multiple strings on a single fret of the guitar.

Barre: Pressing multiple strings across a single fret.

Bass line: A part that emphasizes the roots of a chord progression, often through the repetition of a rhythmic pattern.

Bell: The raised center section of a cymbal.

Belting: A vocal technique for singers where the singer mixes their lower and upper voices, resulting in a sound that resembles yelling but is actually a controlled, sustained phonation.

Bidirectional microphone: A microphone that captures sound equally from either side, in a figure 8 pattern.

Bleed: The sound of one instrument or voice is heard in another track.

Bow: The main surface of a cymbal, in between the edge and raised center.

Capo: A device used to hold down strings across a fret on the guitar.

Cardioid microphone: Features a heart-shaped pattern that mostly captures a sound source directly in front of the microphone.

Channel strip: A series of components, including a preamp and signal processing units (e.g., panning, EQ), designed to integrate a line-level signal from a microphone, electric instrument, or direct box into a mixing console.

Chord chart: A notation system that provides the player with the chord progression and form of the song.

Chord diagram: A representation of the fretboard of a guitar, with dots that indicate finger placement.

Chord progression: A succession of chords. Many popular music songs use the same chord progression.

Close miking: Placing a microphone within two feet of the sound source.

Cloud: A network of internet servers. Cloud-based programs may be accessed from any device connected to the internet, provided it is compatible with the app or software application.

Combo amp: Contains an amplifier and one or more speakers in the same cabinet.

Comping: An original chordal or rhythmic accompaniment that complements the melody.

Condenser microphone: More often used in recording studios than live settings, this type of microphone contains an electrically charged diaphragm that converts the sound to a signal. These microphones are more sensitive than dynamic microphones, capturing more subtleties of the sound source and a wider range of frequencies.

Control room: A separate space from the tracking room, that houses the DAW. Audio engineers can monitor a recording session or edit recorded material in a control room.

Cultural appropriation: The unacknowledged or inappropriate adoption of the customs, practices, ideas, etc. of one people or society by members of another and typically more dominant people or society.

Cypher: A group of rappers, beatboxers, breakdancers, or onlookers, often in a circle, making music alone or together, often as a freestyle.

Diaphragm: A dome-shaped muscular partition separating the thorax from the abdomen. It plays a major role in breathing, as its contraction increases the volume of the thorax and so inflates the lungs.

Differentiation: Designing activities that allow for varying levels of abilities in the classroom.

Digital audio workstation (DAW): A software application or piece of hardware that allows users to record, edit, and mix audio and MIDI (e.g., GarageBand, Audacity, FruityLoops/FL Studio, Soundtrap, Pro Tools, and Logic).

Direct box: A tool that converts instrument signals (often with a 1/4 connection) to be compatible with the microphone input (often with an XLR connection) on a mixing console.

Distant miking: Placing a microphone more than two feet away from the sound source.

DJ/deejay: An abbreviation for Disc Jockey. A person who selects and plays music over a sound system.

Drum sequencer: An electronic device or software for storing sequences of percussion sounds, drum beats, and patterns.

Dynamic microphone: A versatile microphone that is well suited to handle loud volumes. It may be used in live performances as well as recording studios. A dynamic microphone contains a wire coil and magnet that converts sound into an electrical signal.

Effects pedal: An electronic device that alters the sounds of an instrument or other sound source.

Electronic drum kit: An instrument with pads that can trigger a variety of sounds.

EQ: Short for equalization, EQ controls the amount of low, middle, and high frequencies in a signal.

Fader: A sliding rectangular tool that controls the level of the channel.

Feedback: A noise that results from a sound source looping itself through a microphone and nearby speaker or monitor.

Finger tapping: Note generated by tapping the fretboard behind a fret with your nonfretting hand.

Freestyling: The improvisational recitation of lyrics, used often in hip hop.

Frets: Raised metal or plastic strips that separate the neck of an instrument into intervals.

Gobos: Movable walls that create separation between instruments and minimize bleed.

Hammer-on: The action of striking the string with a fretting finger to create a sound on a stringed instrument.

Hybrid ensemble: An ensemble that includes any combination of acoustic, electric, or computer-based instruments. Also known as flexible ensemble, this instrumentation is often drawn from what students bring to the classroom and is not standardized.

Iconic notation: According to the NAfME Core Arts Music Standards Glossary, iconic notation is a representation of sound and its treatment using lines, drawings, and pictures.

Informal learning: An approach to music teaching and learning promoted by Lucy Green. Students choose the music they want to perform, copy recordings by ear, and refine material through individual practice and peer instruction.

Larynx: The hollow muscular organ forming an air passage to the lungs and holding the vocal cords in humans and other mammals; the voice box.

Latency: The time it takes to process an audio signal and send it to the headphones or monitors.

Lead sheet: Notation that provides information about the song, including harmonies (chords), rhythms, lyrics, and melodies.

Main outputs: Final stereo output that includes all the channels and effects. The main output usually connects to speakers or a recording device.

Mastering: A process by which students ensure the dynamic level and equalization of each song is balanced and consistent.

MC/emcee: An abbreviation for Master of Ceremonies. A person who speaks or raps on a microphone over music.

MIDI: An acronym for Musical Instrument Digital Interface. MIDI describes the communication process between a variety of electronic devices (drum pad controller, keyboard controller) and a device that contains a bank of MIDI sounds (e.g., computer sound card). MIDI instruments do not make a sound without the aid of a synthesizer or computer.

Mix (noun): The result of multiple recorded tracks (or live performance tracks) sounding together.

Mix (verb): To balance the individual tracks into a complete whole.

Modern band: A stream of music education that utilizes popular music instruments and music selected and/or written by students.

Monitor (noun): A speaker that plays audio as it is recorded or performed live.

Monitor (verb): To hear audio as it is transmitted during a recording or live performance.

Multitrack recording: The process of recording multiple channels, or tracks, of discrete sounds at the same time.

Omnidirectional microphone: Microphones with a pattern that captures sound from every direction.

Open chord: A chord on the guitar that uses open strings. Also called "cowboy chords."

Panning (or pan): Placing tracks in the left, center, or right side of the mix. This will influence which speaker(s) will sound the track, and to what degree.

Parody: The imitation of the style of a particular song, artist, or genre.

Passive speakers: Speakers that require a separate amplifier to boost the strength of a signal coming from the outputs of a mixer. Passive speakers are generally lighter and less expensive than powered speakers.

Patch: A sound preset for the keyboard, synthesizer, DAW, drum pad, even guitar amp, or pedals OR a term used to describe the process of routing or rerouting the signal in an audio system.

Phantom power (+48v): A 48-volt charge that powers condenser microphones.

Phonation: The production of speech sounds.

Pick: A small flat tool used to pluck or strum a stringed instrument.

Popular music pedagogies: A range of approaches to teaching popular music styles and genres, including informal learning and nonformal teaching practices.

Popular music: Music of the students. In K-12 contexts, this can include currently popular music, student songwriting, folk music, and music that is not commercially popular but is interesting to students.

Power chord: Two- or three-note guitar chords featuring the root and 5th.

Powered speakers: Speakers that feature a built-in amplifier and may be connected directly to the output of the mixer.

Proximity effect: Bass frequencies will increase as the microphone is placed closer to the sound source.

Pull-off: A technique used on a fretted string that is already ringing. By lightly "pulling" the string while removing the finger holding down the note, a new note can be played without picking the string again.

Quantization: Adjusts all of the MIDI data according to a specified note duration (e.g., quarter note, eighth note, sixteenth note).

Riff: A repeated chord progression, pattern, or melody.

Rim: The edge of a cymbal.

Scream singing: An extended vocal technique that is mostly popular in "aggressive" music genres such as heavy metal, punk rock, and noise music.

Signal flow: How signals travel between pieces of audio equipment in a chain (e.g., from the microphone through an audio interface to a computer, back through an interface and out to a pair of headphones).

Simplified chord: Chords that use fewer notes and will be easier to play (e.g., chords using only three strings, and/or one finger on the guitar).

Singing range: The range of pitches that the human voice can phonate.

Slash notation: Slash symbols are used to indicate the number (and sometimes groupings) of beats in a measure.

Slide: A guitar, ukulele, or bass technique in which the player performs one fretted note and then slides the fretting hand up or down the instrument to connect to another pitch, resulting in a glissando.

Slogan: Also known as a "catch phrase," a short expression placed at the end of an improvised line while rapping.

Stereo miking: Using two (or more) microphones to capture the different sounds a listener would hear through the left and right ear.

String bending: A technique for fretted instruments where you "bend" the string up or down on the fretboard to alter the pitch of the played note.

Strumming pattern: A visual representation of the rhythm of chords being strummed on a guitar.

Super cardioid microphone: Features a pattern that captures the sound source directly in front of the microphone, with greater depth and not as much width as a cardioid microphone. Also known as hypercardioid or hyperdirectional.

Sustain pedal: A pedal on the keyboard or piano which "sustains" the sound by moving the dampers away from the strings and allowing them to vibrate freely (or simulating that effect on the keyboard).

Synthesizer: An electronic musical instrument, typically operated by a keyboard, which produces a variety of sounds.

Tablature: A form of notation which indicates the string and fret that should be played. Used primarily for guitar and bass.

Throne: A seat for the drummer sometimes referred to as a stool.

Touch-sensitive key: An effect available on some keyboards that produces louder sounds when the keys are pressed harder, and softer sounds when the keys are pressed softly.

Tracking room: Also known as a live room, this is the space where instrumentalists and vocalists record. It may have acoustic treatments that enhance the quality of the sound.

Tracking: Recording the individual tracks for a project.

Trim knob: Usually placed at the top of a channel strip, a trim knob adjusts the volume (gain) of a signal.

Tuning key: Also referred to as machine heads or tuning pegs, they are the knobs on the headstock of a string instrument that allow you to adjust the pitch of the string by turning the knob and tightening or loosening the string.

Virtual ensemble: An ensemble that does not exist in a physical space, but is created through digital processes or networks.

Virtual instruments: Software-based sounds that may be performed by playing a mobile device or MIDI controller as an instrument.

Vocal register: A range of tones in the human voice produced by a particular vibratory pattern of the vocal folds.

Vocal tessitura: The most acceptable and comfortable vocal range for a given singer or the range in which a given type of voice presents its best-sounding (or characteristic) timbre.

Walking bass line: A progression of notes that outlines the chord progression.

Weighted key: A function on some keyboards that provides slight resistance when pressing down the keys to mimic the feel of an acoustic piano.

BIBLIOGRAPHY

Chapter 1

Allsup, Randall Everett. "Another Perspective: Our 'Both/And' Moment." *Music Educators Journal* 102, no. 2 (2015): 85.

Allsup, Randall Everett, and Eric Shieh. "Social Justice and Music Education: The Call for a Public Pedagogy." *Music Educators Journal* 98, no. 4 (2012): 47–51.

Bowman, Wayne. " 'Pop' Goes…? Taking Popular Music Seriously." In *Bridging the Gap: Popular Music and Music Education*, edited by Carlos Xavier Rodriguez, 29–49. Lanham, MD: Rowman & Littlefield Publishing Group, 2004.

Choate, Robert A., ed. 1968. *Documentary Report of the Tanglewood Symposium: Music in American Society, Lenox, MA, July 23–August 2, 1967.* Washington, DC: Music Educators National Conference.

Corenblum, Barry, and Eric Marshall. "The Band Played on: Predicting Students' Intentions to Continue Studying Music." *Journal of Research in Music Education* 46, no. 1 (1998): 128–140.

Cremata, Radio. "Facilitation in Popular Music Education." *Journal of Popular Music Education* 1, no. 1 (2017): 63–82.

Culp, Mara, and Matthew Clauhs. "Factors that Affect Participation in Secondary School Music: Reducing Barriers and Increasing Access." *Music Educators Journal* 106, no. 4 (2020).

DeLorenzo, Lisa C., ed. *Giving Voice to Democracy in Music Education: Diversity and Social Justice.* New York: Routledge, 2016.

DeLorenzo, Lisa C. "Missing Faces from the Orchestra: An Issue of Social Justice?" *Music Educators Journal* 98, no. 4 (2012): 39–46.

Elliott, David James. *Music Matters: A New Philosophy of Music Education.* New York: Oxford University Press, 1995.

Elpus, Kenneth, and Carlos R. Abril. "High School Music Ensemble Students in the United States: A Demographic Profile." *Journal of Research in Music Education* 59, no. 2 (2011): 128–145.

Elpus, Kenneth, and Carlos R. Abril. "Who Enrolls in School Music? A National Profile of US Students, 2009–2013." *Journal of Research in Music Education* 67, no. 3 (2019): 323–340.

"High School Music Ensemble Students in the United States: A New National Profile." Paper presented at the National Association for Music Education Music Research and Teacher Education National Conference, Atlanta, GA, March 2018.

Fowler, Charles B. "The Case Against Rock: A Reply." *Music Educators Journal* 57, no. 1 (1970): 38–40.

Green, Lucy. *How Popular Musicians Learn: A Way Ahead for Music Education.* Farnham, UK: Ashgate Publishing, 2017.

Green, Lucy. *Music Education as Critical Theory and Practice: Selected Essays.* Farnham: Ashgate, 2014.

Green, Lucy. "Popular Music Education in and for Itself, and for 'Other' Music: Current Research in the Classroom." *International Journal of Music Education* 24, no. 2 (2006): 101–118.

Kerchner, Jody L., and Katherine Strand, eds. *Musicianship: Composing in Choir.* Chicago, IL: GIA Publications, 2016.

Kinney, Daryl W. "Selected Nonmusic Predictors of Urban Students' Decisions to Enroll and Persist in Middle School Band Programs." *Journal of Research in Music Education* 57, no. 4 (2010): 334–350.

Klinedust, Richard E. "Predicting Performance Achievement and Retention of Fifth-Grade Instrumental Students." *Journal of Research in Music Education* 39, no. 3 (1991): 225–238.

Koza, Julia Eklund. "'Save the Music'? Toward Culturally Relevant, Joyful, and Sustainable School Music." *Philosophy of Music Education Review* 14, no. 1 (2006): 23–38.

Kratus, John. "Music Education at the Tipping Point." *Music Educators Journal* 94, no. 2 (2007): 42–48.

Ladson-Billings, Gloria. "Toward a Theory of Culturally Relevant Pedagogy." *American Educational Research Journal* 32, no. 3 (1995): 465–491.

McCarthy, James F. "Individualized Instruction, Student Achievement, and Dropout in an Urban Elementary Instrumental Music Program." *Journal of Research in Music Education* 28, no. 1 (1980): 59–69.

Musical Futures Australia. "An Approach to Learning and Playing Music in the Classroom." 2015. Accessed June 1, 2020. www.musicalfuturesaustralia.org/uploads/1/2/0/1/12012511/informal_learning_normal_teaching_presentation.pdf.

Olesko, Beatrice, "Reconciling Authority and Autonomy: Perspectives of General Music Professors on Democratic Practices in Music Teacher Education." PhD diss., Kent State University, 2020.

Randles, Clint, and David Andrew Stringham, eds. *Musicianship: Composing in Band and Orchestra.* Chicago, IL: GIA Publications, 2013.

Randles, Clint. "Disruptive Performance Technologies." In *The Routledge Research Companion to Music, Technology, and Education*, edited by Andrew King, Evangelos Himonides, and S. Alex Ruthmann, 431–440. New York: Routledge, 2017.

Randles, Clint. "Music Teacher as Writer and Producer." *Journal of Aesthetic Education* 46, no. 3 (2012): 36–52.

Rodriguez, Carlos Xavier, ed. *Bridging the Gap: Popular Music and Music Education.* Lanham, MD: Rowman & Littlefield Publishing Group, 2004.

Schmid, W., and H. March. "The Guide to Teaching with Popular Music." *The National Association for Music Education* (2002).

Weston, Donna. "The Place of Practice in Tertiary Popular Music Studies: An Epistemology." *Journal of Popular Music Education* 1, no. 1 (2017): 101–116.

Woodward, Sheila C. "Social Justice and Popular Music Education: Building a Generation of Artists Impacting Social Change." In *The Routledge Research Companion to Popular Music Education*, edited by Gareth Dylan Smith, Zack Moir, Matt Brennan, Shara Rambarran, and Phil Kirkman, 395–411. New York: Routledge, 2017.

Woody, Robert H. "Popular Music in School: Remixing the Issues." *Music Educators Journal* 93, no. 4 (2007): 32–37.

Chapter 2

NAfME. "Core Music Standards Glossary." Accessed November 20, 2018. https://nafme.org/wp-content/files/2014/06/Core-Music-Standards-Glossary.pdf.

Chapter 3

NAMM. "Global Report." Accessed June 1, 2020. www.namm.org/membership/global-report.

Chapter 7

Smith, Gareth Dylan. *Sound Advice for Drummers*. Verona, NJ: CreateSpace Independent Publishing Platform, 2017.

Chapter 8

American Academy of Teachers of Singing. "In Support of Contemporary Commercial Music (Non-Classical) Voice Pedagogy." *Journal of Voices* 65, no. 1 (2008): 7–10.

Bartlett, Irene. "One Size Doesn't Fit All: Tailored Training for Contemporary Commercial Singers." In *Perspectives on Teaching Singing: Australian Vocal Pedagogues Sing Their Stories*, edited by S. D. Harrison, 227–243. Brisbane: Australian Academic Press, 2010.

Bartlett, Irene. "Reflections on Contemporary Commercial Singing: An Insider's Perspective." *Voice and Speech Review* 8, no. 1 (2014): 27–35.

Björkner, Eva. "Musical Theatre and Opera Singing – Why So Different? A Study of Subglottal Pressure, Voice Source, and Formant Frequency Characteristics." *Journal of Voice* 29, no. 5 (2008): 533–540. https://doi.org/10.1016/j.jvoice.2006.12.007.

Burns, P. "Acoustical Analysis of the Underlying Voice Differences Between Two Groups of Professional Singers: Opera and Country and Western." *The Laryngoscope* 96, no. 5 (1986): 549–554.

Davids, Julia, and Stephen LaTour. "Singing in Tune." Vocal Technique. Accessed January 15, 2020. www.vocaltechnique.info/singing-in-tune.html.

Demorest, Steven M., and Ann Clements. "Factors Influencing the Pitch-Matching of Junior High Boys." *Journal of Research in Music Education* 55, no. 3 (2007): 190–203.

Edwin, R. "Belting: Bel Canto or Brutto Canto?" *Journal of Singing* 59, no. 1 (2002): 67–68.

Harrell, Joey. "Investigation of Current Research Examining the Physiological Differences Between Musical Theatre and Classical Singing: Considerations for Voice Practitioners Training Aspiring Musical Theatre Performers." Unpublished, 2018.

Harris, M. "History and Significance of the Emic/Etic Distinction." *Annual Review of Anthropology* 5, (1976): 329–350.

Hearns, Liz Jackson, and Brian Kremer. *The Singing Teacher's Guide to Transgender Voices*. San Diego, CA: Plural Publishing, 2018.

Kelley, Caitlin. "The Music Industry Still Has a Long Way to Go for Gender Equality." Forbes. Forbes Magazine, April 28, 2019. www.forbes.com/sites/caitlinkelley/2019/02/06/music-industry-study-annenberg-gender-equality/#228ba225f81f.

LeBorgne, Wendy DeLeo, and Marci Daniels Rosenberg. The Vocal Athlete. San Diego, CA: Plural Publishing, 2021.

Nichols, Bryan E. "Task-Based Variability in Children's Singing Accuracy." *Journal of Research in Music Education* 64, no. 3 (2016): 309–321.

Radinoff, S. L. "Artistic Vocal Styles and Techniques." In *The Performer's Voice*, edited by M. Benninger and T. Murry, 51–59. San Diego, CA: Plural Publishing, 2006.

Rutkowski, Joanne, and Martha Snell Miller. "The Effect of Teacher Feedback and Modeling on First Graders' Use of Singing Voice and Developmental Music Aptitude." *Bulletin of the Council for Research in Music Education*, no. 156 (2003): 1–10.

Saunders-Barton, Mary. "Bel Canto/Can Belto: Musical Theatre Singing for Women, Vocalises for the Flexible Vocal Tract." Used by permission. Accessed June 1, 2020. www.nats.org/_Library/Winter_Workshop_NYC_2018/FEMALE_VOCALISES_Mary_Sauders-Barton.pdf.

Soto-Morettini, Donna. *Popular Singing and Style*. 2nd ed. London: Bloomsbury Publishing, 2014.

Spivey, N. "Music Theatre Singing … Let's Talk. Part 2: Examining the Debate on Belting." *Journal of Singing* 64, no. 5 (2008): 607–611.

Thalen, M., and J. Sundberg. "Describing Different Styles of Singing: A Comparison of a Female Singer's Voice Source in 'Classical', 'Pop', 'Jazz' and 'Blues.'" *Logopedics Phoniatrics Vocology* 26, no. 2 (2001): 82–93.

"Voice Disorders." American Speech-Language-Hearing Association. Accessed January 15, 2020. www.asha.org/PRPSpecificTopic.aspx?folderid=8589942600&section=Causes.

Welch, G. F., E. Himonides, I. Papageorgi, J. Saunders, T. Rinta, C. Stewart, C. Preti, J. Lani, M. Vraka, and J. Hill. "The National Singing Programme for Primary Schools in England: An Initial Baseline Study." *Music Education Research* 11, no. 1 (2009): 1–22.

Chapter 9

Byo, Susan J. "Classroom Teachers' and Music Specialists' Perceived Ability to Implement the National Standards for Music Education." *Journal of Research in Music Education* 47, no. 2 (1999): 111–123.

Cremata, Radio, Pignato, J. M., Powell, B., and Smith, G. D. The Music Learning Profiles Project: Let's Take This Outside. New York: Routledge, 2017.

Eddins, John M. "A Brief History of Computer-Assisted Instruction in Music." *College Music Symposium* 21, no. 2 (1981): 7–14.

Kladder, J. "The Non-Traditional Secondary Music Performance Class." In *The Learner-Centered Classroom*, edited by David Williams and Jonathan Kladder, 141–160. New York: Routledge, 2020.

"National Core Arts Standards." Accessed May 24, 2017. www.nationalartsstandards.org/.

"National Core Arts Standards: A Conceptual Framework for Arts Learning." Accessed December 31, 2017. www.nationalartsstandards.org/sites/default/files/Conceptual%20Framework%2007-21-16.pdf.

Rideout, Victoria J., and Vikki S. Katz. Opportunity for All? Technology and Learning in Lower-Income Families. A Report of the Families and Media Project. New York: The Joan Ganz Cooney Center at Sesame Workshop, 2016.

Waldrop, M. Mitchell. "The Chips are Down for Moore's Law." *Nature News* 530, no. 7589 (2016): 144.

Williams, David A. "Another Perspective: The iPad is a REAL Musical Instrument." *Music Educators Journal* 101, no. 1 (2014): 93–98.

Chapter 10

Chen, Brian X. "Indie Musicians Record Entire Album with GarageBand for iPad." April 4, 2011. www.wired.com/gadgetlab/2011/04/indie-band-ipad.

Clauhs, Matthew, Brian Franco, and Radio Cremata. "Mixing It Up: Sound Recording and Music Production in School Music Programs." *Music Educators Journal* 106, no. 1 (2019): 55–63.

Kettering, Charles V. "The Recording Procedure in Music Education." *Music Educators Journal* 22, no. 5 (1936): 29–84.

Rainie, Lee, and Andrew Perrin. "10 Facts About Smartphones as the iPhone Turns 10." *Pew Research Center* (2017).

Chapter 11

Clauhs, Matthew, Brian Franco, and Radio Cremata. "Mixing It Up: Sound Recording and Music Production in School Music Programs." *Music Educators Journal* 106, no. 1 (2019): 55–63.

Randles, Clint. "Music Teacher as Writer and Producer." *Journal of Aesthetic Education* 46, no. 3 (2012): 36–52.

Chapter 12

Cayari, Christopher. "Virtual Vocal Ensembles and the Mediation of Performance on YouTube." PhD diss., University of Illinois at Urbana-Champaign, 2016.

Clauhs, Matthew, and Radio Cremata. "Student Voice and Choice in Modern Band Curriculum Development." *Journal of Popular Music Education* 4, no. 1 (2020): 101–116.

Green, Lucy. *How Popular Musicians Learn: A Way Ahead for Music Education.* Farnham, UK: Ashgate Publishing, 2017.

Hallam, Susan, and Andrea Creech. *Music Education in the 21st Century in the United Kingdom: Achievements, Analysis and Aspirations.* Institute of Education, University of London, 2010.

Isbell, Daniel S. "Music Educators Consider Musical Futures: Professional Development in the United Kingdom." *Contributions to Music Education* 43, (2018): 39–58.

Marvuglio, Matt, and Jonathan Feist. *Berklee Practice Method Teacher's Guide: Get Your Band Together.* Boston, MA: Berklee Press Publications, 2004.

Powell, Bryan, and Scott Burstein. "Popular Music and Modern Band Principles." In *The Routledge Research Companion to Popular Music Education*, edited by Gareth Dylan Smith, Zack Moir, Matt Brennan, Shara Rambarran, and Phil Kirkman, 244–245. New York: Routledge, 2017.

Powell, Bryan. "A Zero-Sum Game? Modern Band's Impact on Student Enrollment in Traditional Music Ensembles." *School Music News-New York State School Music Association* (2019): 20–23.

"Role of the Lead Vocalist." Vocalist.org.uk. Accessed January 15, 2020. www.vocalist.org.uk/lead_vocalist.html.

Tobias, Evan. "Hybrid Spaces and Hyphenated Musicians: Secondary Students' Musical Engagement in a Songwriting and Technology Course." *Music Education Research* 14, no. 3 (2012): 329–346.

Chapter 13

Axis of Awesome. "Axis of Awesome – 4 Four Chord Song (with song titles)." Network Ten Australia. December 10, 2009. Video, 5:30. https://bit.ly/2vw4oR3.

Kerchner, Jody L., and Katherine Strand, eds. *Musicianship: Composing in Choir.* Chicago, IL: GIA Publications, 2016.

NAfME. "Standards." Accessed March 29, 2020. https://nafme.org/my-classroom/standards/.

Randles, Clint, and David Andrew Stringham, eds. *Musicianship: Composing in Band and Orchestra.* Chicago, IL: GIA Publications, 2013.

Wish, David, G. Heimbauer, C. Speicher, J. Flora, A. DiMasso, R. Zellner, and S. Danielsson. *Music as a Second Language and the Modern Band Movement.* Verona, NJ: Little Kids Rock, 2016.

Chapter 14

Campbell, Patricia Shehan. *Teaching Music Globally.* Oxford University Press, 2004.

Chang, Jeff. *Can't Stop Won't Stop: A History of the Hip-Hop Generation.* New York: St. Martin's Press, 2005.

Clauhs, Matthew, and Radio Cremata. "Student Voice and Choice in Modern Band Curriculum Development." *Journal of Popular Music Education* 4, no. 1 (2020): 101–116.

Green, Lucy. *How Popular Musicians Learn: A Way Ahead for Music Education.* Farnham, UK: Ashgate Publishing, 2017.

Green, Lucy. "What Can Music Educators Learn from Popular Musicians?" In *Bridging the Gap: Popular Music and Music Education*, edited by Carlos Xavier Rodrigues, 225–241. Lanham, MD: Rowman & Littlefield Publishing Group, 2004.

Guo, Jeff. "How Iggy Azalea Mastered Her 'Blaccent'." *The Washington Post*, Jan. 4, 2016. www.washingtonpost.com/news/wonk/wp/2016/01/04/how-a-white-australian-rapper-mastered-her-blaccent/.

Hess, Juliet. "Popular Music Education: A Way Forward or a New Hegemony?" In *The Bloomsbury Handbook of Popular Music Education: Perspectives and Practices*, edited by Zack Moir, Bryan Powell, and Gareth Dylan Smith, 30. London: Bloomsbury Publishing, 2019.

Pennington, Rosemary. "Dissolving the Other: Orientalism, Consumption, and Katy Perry's Insatiable Dark Horse." *Journal of Communication Inquiry* 40, no. 2 (2016): 111–127.

RBR-TVBR. "Hip-Hop, Consumers and Retail." *Radio and Television Business Report*, March 22, 2012. www.rbr.com/hip-hop-consumers-and-retail/.

Serjeant, Jill. "Hip Hop and R&B Surpass Rock as Biggest U.S. Music Genre." *Reuters*, Jan. 4, 2018. www.reuters.com/article/us-music-2017/hip-hop-and-rb-surpass-rock-as-biggest-u-s-music-genre-idUSKBN1ET258.

Wish, David, G. Heimbauer, C. Speicher, J. Flora, A. DiMasso, R. Zellner, and S. Danielsson. "Hip Hop Hamburger," accessed June 1, 2020. http://jamzone.cdn.littlekidsrock.org/wp-content/uploads/2016/09/LP_Songwriting-HipHopHamberger-Worksheets.pdf.

Woodward, Sheila C. "Social Justice and Popular Music Education: Building a Generation of Artists Impacting Social Change." In *The Routledge Research Companion to Popular Music Education*, edited by Gareth Dylan Smith, Zack Moir, Matt Brennan, Shara Rambarran, and Phil Kirkman, 395–411. New York: Routledge, 2017.

INDEX

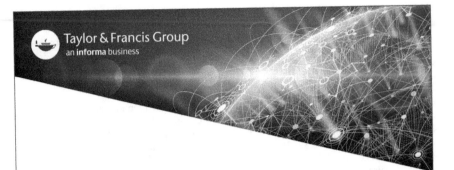

Printed in the USA
CPSIA information can be obtained
at www.ICGtesting.com
CBHW072212230824
13662CB00008B/535

9 780367 266585